HIDDEN LANDSCAPES OF THE

SOUTH WEST COAST PATH

HIDDEN LANDSCAPES OF THE
SOUTH WEST
COAST PATH

WALK  EXPLORE  DISCOVER

RUTH LUCKHURST

HALSGROVE

First published in Great Britain in 2016

*Title page photograph: George Burt's huge limestone globe at Durlston Castle
is one of many Victorian monuments on the coastline*

British Library Cataloguing-in-Publication Data
A CIP record for this title is available from the British Library

ISBN 978 0 85704 283 5

HALSGROVE
Halsgrove House,
Ryelands Industrial Estate,
Bagley Road, Wellington, Somerset TA21 9PZ
Tel: 01823 653777   Fax: 01823 216796
email: sales@halsgrove.com

Part of the Halsgrove group of companies
Information on all Halsgrove titles is available at: www.halsgrove.com

Printed and bound in China by Everbest Printing Investment Ltd

Contents

FOREWORD

By South West Coast Path National Trail Officer Mark Owen

ANYONE WHO LOVES walking the South West Coast Path National Trail and wants to find out more about the landscapes it passes through and the heritage found along our coastline will enjoy this book. Ruth has done a great job of bringing to life the stories behind the diverse landscapes to be found as you walk around our wonderful peninsula.

For millennia, people have lived, worked, worshipped and occasionally had to fight along the coast line followed by the South West Coast Path. In researching walks for our website, Ruth must have covered thousands of miles, spoken to numerous experts and unearthed material from archives and museums. I'm delighted that through this book, she is able to bring all this together to give an overview of what you'll find as you explore the UK's longest National Trail.

Going back to the underlying geology as Ruth has done, sets the scene to understand how and why people have lived and shaped our coastal landscapes. The rocks also influence where wildlife is found, why villages and towns have sprung up where they did, how the land is farmed, and even the positioning of churches and castles.

I hope that this book encourages you to discover the often hidden places and history to be found along the South West Coast Path – I know it's given me lots of ideas of places I want to go back to, as in previous visits I hadn't spotted things Ruth has written about.

Opposite:
On the Exmoor coastline, Rhododendra planted by the Reverend William Halliday on his Glenthorne estate provide a riot of colour in early summer.

PREFACE

EARLY IN 2010, I had the great fortune to be commissioned to write 235 short circular walks based on the South West Coast Path, part of the major project funded by the Rural Development Programme for England, "Unlocking Our Coastal Heritage". With my camera, notebook and tent I set out on what many envious walkers acclaimed as "the best job in the world", and I was very quickly seduced by the romance of the region's coastline.

The work evolved as businesses requested Coast Path walks starting near them, and in the next four years I wrote more than 500 walks. The pressures of the project meant that I wasn't able to sit around waiting for good weather, and there were times when I was wading through mud or hanging on to fences for fear of being blown over cliffs; but the South West coastline never once lost its magic for me.

This book isn't about the scenery, which is there for all to see, nor is there much about its wildlife, which deserves a volume to itself. It doesn't mention buses, B&Bs, real ale or dog walks – southwestcoastpath.org.uk has all the practical information that walkers need, as well as the full collection of walks funded by the project.

This is the story of the coastal landscape, from when its first rocks were laid down on an ancient seabed, 600 million years ago, to the dawn of the era that emerged at the end of the Second World War. It describes how the land was spectacularly sculpted by the collision of continents, and how time, weather and the massive power of the sea have continued to reshape it since. It introduces the people whose lives revolved around their relationship with the sea during the last 300,000 years, and it touches on the way they in turn have affected the landscape around them.

I have done my best to check the accuracy of the facts, but the breadth of the subject means that there will be errors, especially given that even experts are unable to agree on some of the topics. When it comes to giants, mermaids and anything to do with King Arthur, I haven't let facts get in the way of a good story, but the discerning reader will easily identify these lapses.

Opposite:
A place of windswept trees and ancient stone crosses, the churchyard at Lelant sits on the ancient overland route used by sea fareres to avoid the tracherous waters around Land's End.

Great swathes of the region have been designated special areas for their geology, wildlife or heritage: Sites of Special Scientific Interest, Special Conservation Areas, Areas of Outstanding Natural Beauty, Heritage Coasts, World Heritage Sites, a Geopark – the list is endless – but details of these are readily available elsewhere, and I haven't included them here. Nor have I lingered on the history of large coastal towns; and I have failed to mention innumerable lighthouses, shipwreck sites, pillboxes, barrows and rockfaces along the Coast Path's 630 miles. Full details of every one of these, and plenty more, can be found in the walks on the South West Coast Path website and in further titles planned for the future: this is just a taster.

Throughout the project I was given the unstinting support of the passionate and knowledgeable army of people who protect and promote the Coast Path, from rangers to archivists, and my heartfelt thanks go to all of them. Special mention goes to South West Coast Path National Trail Officer Mark Owen and his team; guidebook writer Paddy Dillon; Nick Hallissey of Country Walking; Dave Edgcumbe of North Devon AONB; Emma Trevarthen of Cornwall & Scilly Historic Environment Record; Andy Simmons, Mike Simmonds and Paul Camp of the National Trust; Jenny Penney of Dorset Countryside Service; Phil Chambers of Dawlish Warren Nature Reserve; Pat Wilson of the English Riviera Geopark; Lesley Dalladay, for the photo of a chough; and the many kind souls in the region's campsites who invited me into their homes and motorhomes to dry off/warm up/have breakfast/hear their own stories of walking the Coast Path.

Opposite:
Behind Port Quinn's mineral-stained rocks and caves, the pilchard cellars and ruined fishermen's cottages tell the sad tale of "the village that died twice". A Viking longboat is said to be buried beneath the sand.

1
ONCE UPON A TIME…

545 MILLION YEARS ago there was no Atlantic Ocean, and England and Scotland were on separate continents. Most of the South West was at the bottom of a sea, where thick layers of mud and sand were deposited. Over time these were compressed into mudstones and sandstones, and conglomerates formed as grit and pebbles were embedded in the seabed sediments. There were several orogenies – periods of mountain-building, caused by high-impact collisions between the continental plates churning on the Earth's surface, generating enormous heat and pressure and dramatically altering the shape and structure of their rocks.

The Lizard peninsula is one of the few places where rocks this old can still be seen. They were laid down at the bottom of the Rheic Ocean around 600 million years ago, although they would not reach the surface for another few hundred million years.

In time primitive marine species materialised and started to diversify, developing new ways of moving and protecting themselves. Shells appeared on some of the soft-bodied species, giving rise to fossils in the rocks. A few animals and plants ventured towards the shore, but there was no life on land yet. The climate was cool, although the shallow sea that covered much of the land was beginning to warm up. Around 450 million years ago, the continent known as Gondwana started to break up, and England drifted north on a small plate known as Avalonia.

As Gondwana drifted back towards the South Pole, a 500,000-year ice age began. The massive ice sheet in the southern hemisphere locked up much of the Earth's water, causing a drop in sea level and wiping out 85% of marine life.

Later a series of continental collisions triggered the Caledonian orogeny, and England and Scotland were shunted together to form the British Isles. The margins of Southern England disappeared beneath a shallow sea as the ice sheets melted and sea levels rose again. The creation of reefs provided a new ecosystem, and marine species now included sponges, corals and sea lilies, as well as the very first bony fish. Britain was drifting north again, but it was still over 20° south of the Equator and its climate was almost tropical. The first plant colonies grew on dry land, and the earliest wetland habitats formed as some species grew along the margins of rivers and lakes.

Opposite:
WOODY BAY COASTAL WATERFALL
On the Exmoor coastline, water draining from the high moorland above has carved narrow gullies, known locally as combes. Woody Bay's waterfall plunges to the southern shoreline of the Old Red Sandstone continent. A short distance west, Hollowbrook's cascade marks the faultline where the first Devonian rocks were laid down beneath the shallow sea lapping on the Old Red.

THE DEVONIAN PERIOD

At the start of the Devonian period, Britain was part of the Old Red Sandstone landmass. Coloured red by rich deposits of iron oxide, the continent also included Europe, North America and Greenland, and it lay 10° south of the Equator. Sea levels were higher, and the climate was much warmer. The balmy water led to the evolution of several major new fish species, in lakes and rivers too, and the sea teemed with corals and crustaceans. Insects and amphibians appeared, and plants grew ever more sophisticated.

In Southern England, large rivers flowed across extensive coastal plains, carrying sediments washed from the mountains to the north and west. In Somerset, large deltas built these Old Red deposits out into the shallow sea, forming thick sequences of slates and sandstones, and Exmoor, the Mendips, the Quantocks and the Brendon Hills were formed. In the shallow water around North Devon and Exmoor, mudstones, sandstones, shales and some limestones were deposited and compressed into rock strata. Starting with the Lynton Beds at Hollowbrook, layers of slates were laid down to the south, with successively younger strata washed southwards over the top of earlier layers.

HANGMAN GRITS AT GLENTHORNE

The Hangman Grits underlying the Exmoor coastline are dramatically displayed on Glenthorne Beach. Fossils found in the rocks formed from the Old Red sediments show that sea levels were rising. Great Hangman, the highest of the Middle Devonian "hogsback" hills between Combe Martin and Minehead, is also England's highest seacliff, at 318m.

POLZEATH SLATE

Daymer Bay's Polzeath Slate contains particularly good Devonian fossils showing the conditions in which the rocks were laid down, enabling geologists to date them. In Rock Dunes, fringing the bay, a wide range of insects thrives as a result of the unusual species in the maritime grassland, which include the rare sea spurge.

15

Cornwall was still on the edge of the Rheic Ocean, a short distance south of the Old Red. Thick strata of mudstones and limestones were laid down here, too, and beds of Dartmouth slates were deposited coast-to-coast in a band stretching from Start Bay to Watergate Bay, their colour varying from purple to a greenish-grey. The fossils in the fine-grained slates between Polperro and Lantic Bay show shallow-water species.

MULLION ISLAND
Mullion Island marks the faultline where continental plate movement bulldozed Cornwall's Precambrian rocks on to the southern edge of the much younger mainland during the Devonian period. Mullion Island itself, particularly noted for its colonies of nesting seabirds, is a result of lava being thrust through the rocks below the sea by an underwater volcano in the middle of the period.

Later the water deepened in South and East Devon, forming siltstones and limestones. Devonian fossils here show corals living in reefs associated with volcanic islands, and lavas and tuffs were deposited in the deep basin to the south and west of the Old Red. Slates and limestones were laid down around Southern Cornwall, and conglomerates with embedded fragments of the older rocks from the landmass to the south. Between Port Isaac and Padstow, mudstones and limestones were formed in deeper water, with large volumes of volcanic lava being forced into the seabed from below.

WATERSIDE COVE TUFF DYKE
On the South Devon coast, the slates, siltstones and sandstones of the Meadfoot Beds overlying the Dartmouth Slates show signs of later volcanic activity. In Paignton's Waterside Cove, a tuff dyke – looking like a low wall built into the cliff and extended horizontally on to the beach – is actually the solidified remains of volcanic material thrust into cracks in the older rock above it. When the dyke cooled, its constituent rock was much harder than the rock around it, which later eroded, leaving the dyke standing alone.

In Torbay, Middle Devonian limestone in Walls Hill has given rise to a unique type of vegetation known as squill-spurge fescue grasslands. More than thirty rare plants grow here, including the white rock rose, and the many butterflies attracted to their wildflowers include the marbled white. Here the limestone is eroded by rainwater as well as the sea. Being very

BEDRUTHAN STEPS

Bedruthan Steps' Devonian fossils are particularly valuable for dating the rocks. These include a primitive fish with no jaw, known as a pteraspis, and the large plankton-like Pteroconus Mirus, which had bladders to help it float. The spectacular islands, coves and caves on this part of the coastline – so useful later to smugglers – are the result of the sea exploiting faults and fissures in the rock. At Trevone, south of Padstow, there is an enormous crater in the heathland, where the roof of a sea cave finally collapsed. Over time, this will turn into a cove as the sea continues to eat into the rock, and eventually it will become a bay.

slightly acidic, over time the rain dissolves the limestone around the cracks caused by Earth movements, prising chunks apart. Kent's Cavern – famed for its early Stone Age inhabitants – was formed as a result of these processes, as was another bone cave later found at nearby Redgate, no longer accessible.

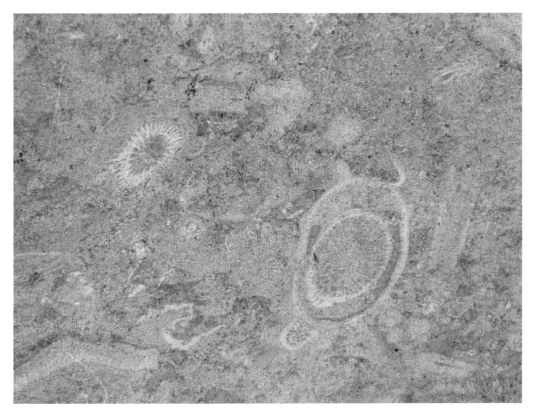

PAIGNTON LIMESTONE FOSSILS
The Torquay limestone used in many buildings around Paignton is rich in Devonian fossils, enabling geologists to identify five different types of this rock. Although they were all laid down at the same time, in the middle of the period, the fossilised species show that this was in five slightly different environments. These fine, pale limestones – excellent for building – have been extensively quarried at Walls Hill, Babbacombe Barton, Berry Head, Hope's Nose and Petit Tor.

Underwater volcanoes in the Upper Devonian period produced the thick pillow lava found at Pentire Point and the Rumps. Here the rocks are peppered with tiny holes where the hot gases bubbled through. South of the Camel estuary, the Longcarrow Cove tuff beds are a result of the same volcanoes. More pillow lava can be seen in the caves at Port Quin, where the surrounding rocks are vividly stained by minerals produced as a result of the great heat.

The Upper Devonian slates laid down around the Tintagel/Boscastle area of North Cornwall were formed in calm waters with few sediments, leading to a fine-grained, smooth slate that is excellent for building, and the fossils found in the limestones deposited with it are particularly well preserved because of the lack of currents.

MORTE POINT

Formed during the Upper Devonian period, the "Devil's Teeth" rocks around Morte Point claimed no fewer than 26 ships in the nineteenth century alone. The rock layers forming this sunken reef were tilted almost vertically during the continental collision at the end of the Carboniferous period. The Normans called it the "Death Stone", saying: "Morte is the place which heaven made last and the devil will take first." At nearby Windy Cove, the cliffs are noted for their "slaty cleavage", where these same Earth movements recrystallised and reorientated the minerals in the mud-rich rocks, meaning that the layers in the slate are more easily split, making them ideal for roofing and tiling.

THE CARBONIFEROUS PERIOD

350 million years ago, the highest oxygen levels ever recorded on Earth encouraged the evolution of the first reptiles. The Carboniferous period is named from the huge quantities of carbon stored in the Earth as a result of the plants that grew and died and were later turned to coal. The start of the period was warm, with higher sea levels, and most of England was under shallow tropical seas rich in marine life.

In Devon, thick sequences of sandstones, shales and mudstones were deposited in a sea basin, with large sheets of lava and ash from widespread volcanic activity. Further south, limestones were formed as well. From time to time swirling currents swept sands and

PENALLY POINT

The Carboniferous rocks around Boscastle's Penally Point were dramatically deformed during the mountain-building episode at the end of the period, which also forced molten minerals into cracks in these rocks. The cliffs were then sculpted by the tremendous power of the Atlantic rollers that pound this coastline. There is an underground roar here – the sound of the sea invading the caves it has carved in the slate – and around low tide, the surge of water through one of these caves erupts in a dramatic spout into Boscastle harbour. There is a similar blowhole at Newquay's Trevelgue Head.

pebbles down the basin walls, possibly as a result of earthquakes. In Cornwall, the Carboniferous Crackington Formation was soon covered over by sandstones, silts and shales from the Bude Formation. At Barras Nose these sedimentary rocks were overlain by tuffs and lavas from the Tintagel Volcanic Formation. These Carboniferous rock sequences are named the Culm Measures, from the soft sooty coal formed here, known as culm.

Gradually the sea levels dropped again and extensive deltas were formed from deposits washed from the Scottish landmass to the north, becoming carpeted with thick forests of giant ferns and horsetails. Eventually Britain's shallow seas drained away completely, leaving broad coastal plains covered in swampy forests. Rivers streamed across the land, shifting course and forming lakes as they went, with great tracts of lush vegetation spread between them. As the leaves, branches and eventually trees themselves fell to the ground, so they were turned to peat. In time the layers of peat were compressed and fossilised and turned to coal.

CULM CLIFFS
The soaring Culm Cliffs near Clovelly are of geological importance for their bands of shale and sandstone. These were spectacularly folded at the end of the period, and then overturned to the north and refolded in a series of much smaller folds dipping eastwards. The underlying rocks give rise to Culm Grassland, a marshy pasture of rushes and moorland grass which supports a wide range of species, including several uncommon orchids and the rare marsh fritillary butterfly.

THE VARISCAN OROGENY

At the end of the Carboniferous Period, the Variscan orogeny formed Europe's mountain ranges, dramatically re-sculpting the landscape and altering the structure of the rocks fronting the collision between the two continents. Around Hartland the shale was baked to slate, hardening it to such an extent that the rivers later flowing over its surface to the sea did not carve out valleys in the rock. The waves pounding the cliffs, however, roll straight in from the North American coastline, and by the time they arrive at Hartland they have gathered considerable force. The result is "hanging valleys", where the rivers reach the sea almost 30m above the beach and plunge to the shoreline below in spectacular waterfalls, like the one at Spekes Mill Mouth.

HARTLAND CLIFFS

At the cutting edge of the plate activity during the Variscan orogeny, the North Cornwall/ Devon coastline was thrust violently upwards into a mountain range whose peaks are thought to have reached 3000m. From Widemouth to Hartland Point, the towering cliffs display vertical strata and dramatic chevrons where the rocks were crumpled by the huge forces at work.

Above:

BABBACOMBE DOLERITE

At the foot of Babbacombe Cliffs there are outcrops of black dolerite, a hard igneous rock intruded into the Devonian rocks during the Variscan orogeny. The dolerite's heat hardened the sandstones and changed the minerals in the limestone, altering its colour. The rock strata were also overturned, so that the mudstones and dark slates of the Babbacombe Shales and the Norden Formation have ended up underneath the older limestone.

Top left:

GOODRINGTON BOUDINAGE

South Devon's Devonian rocks were equally metamorphosed and deformed by the enormous heat and pressure of the Variscan Earth movements. At Goodrington they have been squeezed into a shape known as "boudinage" (French for "sausage").

Bottom left:

TREVOSE ROCKS

Dykes of a rock known as greenstone, formed from dolerite, were intruded into sediments still being consolidated on the Cornish coastline. These sediments were baked hard, making them more resistant to the sea's erosion, resulting in the headland at Trevose Head. Greenstone headlands also occur at Gurnard's Head and Botallack.

COVERACK MOHO

Around 375 million years ago, the rock about to become the Lizard was some 10km beneath the Earth's surface, sitting in a molten layer between the crust and the mantle. Under the tremendous pressures generated by the movement of the plates, this "Moho" layer started making its way up through the crust. As it punched its way through the molten rocks, it brought a complete sequence of them to the surface – igneous rocks, volcanic lava and ocean sediments. Today Coverack beach is one of only three places in Britain where the fossilised Moho layer can be seen. The northern end of the beach is formed of gabbro – a hard rock extensively quarried around the area and used for roadstone – while around the harbour the rocks are serpentine. Between the two, the transition zone features a jumble of both kinds of rocks, as well as basalt and gneiss, also formed below the Earth's surface and altered by the heat and pressure as they were forced through it.

KENNACK DYKE

At Kennack Sands, the rubble of beach boulders includes basalt, serpentine, gneiss, gabbro, bastite – all rocks originating in the Earth's mantle or crust and altered on their way up by the pressure and heat. The cliffs above the beach incorporate spectacular dykes, created when molten rock of one type was forced through the cracks in another. Most noteworthy are the dykes of pink Kennack gneiss, some of which have gathered up chunks of serpentine and embedded them within the gneiss itself. There are other dykes of basalt and gabbro, fringed with asbestos and talc, formed as a result of a chemical reaction between serpentine and basalt.

KYNANCE SERPENTINE

The Lizard is the largest area of serpentine in the country. This was formed from a rock in the Earth's mantle, known as peridotite. As it was forced through the crust, it was transformed into the two different types of serpentine that can be seen on Kynance beach – bastite serpentine, coarse-grained and flecked with large, sparkling crystals; and tremolite, fine-grained and banded because of greater pressure as it rose to the surface. A cliff overhanging the beach shows a mix of both serpentines mangled together. The friction of the collision created a fine network of cracks which was filled by molten minerals including calcite and talc.

"Soapy Cove" – Gew-Graze on the map, between Mullion and Kynance Cove – marks the point where there was once a talc mine, exploiting one of the by-products of the chemical reactions that took place. The rock lies at the bottom of a gully where the schist gives way to the much older serpentine. The different habitats rising from these two discrete rock types can be plainly seen: the water streaming down the gully travels through marshy heathland, while towards Kynance the serpentine has produced a special grassland, teeming with wildflowers.

Another result of the upheavals on the Earth's surface was the dramatic remodelling of southern Cornwall. Five large bodies of granite – known as plutons – were forced upwards through the sedimentary rocks as part of the Earth's crust melted in the huge temperatures. The largest of these plutons stretched from today's Scilly Isles all the way to Dartmoor in a body of granite underlying the whole of southern Cornwall – the Cornubian batholith. The smaller plutons formed surface eruptions on the main batholith, resulting in large granite masses around the Scilly Isles, Land's End and elsewhere inland. Dykes of quartz-porphyry

PORTHCURNO CLIFFS
Around Land's End, the rectangular blocks and soaring buttresses make for a spectacular coastline. Here, despite having been baked hard during the mountain-building episode, the rock has been hammered into towering cliffs and plunging gullies ("zawns") by the sea's massive power. The granite outcrops contain crystals of feldspar whose length shows that the granite cooled down very slowly after it had been intruded.

CHAPEL PORTH CAVE

The minerals in the water circulating through the fissures in the granite resulted in Cornwall's rich tin, copper and tungsten deposits. Further Earth movements some 50 million years later led to the formation of lead, silver, iron and zinc. Around the St Agnes area, the cliffs are stained red by the minerals...

...although there is another explanation, acted out in an open-air pageant every May on the site of the sixth-century St Agnes chapel. The Giant Bolster lived on St Agnes Beacon and passed his time throwing rocks around the landscape. His poor wife, forced to gather these rocks every day and carry them back to him in her apron, became old and haggard long before her time. The faithless giant turned his attentions to young Agnes, whom he'd heard singing in the fields below; but the canny maiden demanded that he prove his love by cutting his arm and filling a small hole at the clifftop with his blood. Being a simple giant, and not understanding that the hole led to a sea cave, he happily agreed. His blood drained out to sea and he fell to his death on the beach below.

– elvan dykes – were formed around the plutons, and one of these can be seen on the beach at Praa Sands. Other similar dykes are visible around Newquay Headland and the Gannel. Smaller outcrops of coarse-grained igneous intrusions formed in the same way, with crystals sometimes several inches long, occur at Cligga Head, near Carbis Bay's Knill Monument and on St Michael's Mount.

SENNEN CHINA CLAY WORKS
One of the last changes in the granite at the end of the orogeny was its "kaolinization", where the movement of acids along joints in the rock changed it into china clay. This occurs primarily around St Austell, where it is commercially exploited for ceramics and glazes, as well as pharmaceutical and other chemical products, using china clay "dries" at Par. Smaller china clay works existed elsewhere, like this one in the heathland above Sennen Cove.

THE PERMIAN PERIOD

At the end of the Carboniferous period the temperature plummeted, and the Earth was plunged into a polar ice age that lasted millions of years. The climate did not warm again until the Permian period began, around 300 million years ago.

After the two colliding landmasses had merged and formed the continent known to geologists as Pangea, things started to quieten down around the plates. Straddling the Equator, Pangea reached both poles and the face of the Earth became a hot, dry desert as ocean circulation systems shifted. Only coastal and north-easterly areas were well-watered, while the rest of the land was subject to monsoons alternating with droughts. The iron in the rocks oxidised, colouring the landscape red, and beds of gypsum and other salts formed as the water evaporated from former lakes.

WATCOMBE CLIFFS
Along the shoreline from Paignton to Seaton, the sandstone laid down in desert conditions during the Permian period lies "unconformably" over older rocks – there was once a layer of rock between them, but it was eroded away before the Permian rock was formed. Near the soaring red cliffs glimpsed through the trees at Watcombe, the missing layer has left kaolinite – china clay associated with granite – producing the clay used in the world-famous Watcombe Pottery.

SHOALSTONE FAULT

At Shoalstone, Permian sandstone was laid down on top of Brixham limestone, some 100 million years after this was formed. Acidic rainwater made its way through the fissures in the limestone, dissolving the rock and widening the cracks. The sandstone forming above sank through the joints that were formed, filling the hollow as it went. Nearby, formations known as "Neptunian dykes" were a result of the same process. When the limestone surrounding a dyke was finally completely eroded, the sandstone was left standing.

Dartmoor, Exmoor, the Mendips and the Quantocks were still mountains; but as these Carboniferous rocks began to erode, vast amounts of sediment were swept across the plains below in episodes of flash flooding. These short-lived torrents deposited thick sequences of red sandstones, conglomerates and breccias.

Most Permian rocks visible today are in Torbay and East Devon, but small outcrops at Slapton and between Bolt Head and Plymouth show that they once covered a considerable area. The red cliffs faulted against the Devonian limestones in Babbacombe and Petit Tor are Permian, and their conglomerates and breccias have clasts of Devonian limestone. There are Permian sandstones at Oddicombe, with outcrops of fine-grained breccias and sandstones between Dawlish and Exmouth. The clasts in Shaldon's Teignmouth Breccia are of quartzite and a quartz porphyry, a volcanic rock formed in association with Dartmoor granite during the Variscan episode.

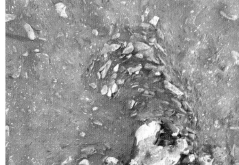

GIANT CENTIPEDE TRACKS

Permian rocks show few signs of life, but on the shoreline near Goodrington there are some remarkable trails of tiny pebbles in the sandstone. Geologists have argued over the nature of these "trace fossils" for many years, but now it is generally agreed that these trails were left by giant centipedes, possibly as long as 10cm (4in), chewing their way through the sand! The Earth's worst-ever episode of extinction happened at the end of the period, with 96% of all species wiped out.

THE TRIASSIC PERIOD

At the start of the Triassic period, 250 million years ago, Britain was on a latitude roughly equivalent to today's Sahara Desert, and even the polar areas were warm and covered in forest. Pangea's surface was still desert, with large braided rivers flowing across the desert plains between the mountains, forming vast tracts of sandstone, breccias and conglomerates. Sediments accumulated in large basins, forming sandstones in dunes and mudstones in shallow lakes.

The rocks were still red and easily eroded. Rivers washing sediment from the high ground deposited it along the Devon coast between Exmouth and Sidmouth, spreading it westwards to underlie much of today's Somerset. There is an isolated outcrop on the beach at Peppercombe, where it lies unconformably on Carboniferous rocks, and Triassic rocks beneath Poole Harbour contain western Europe's largest onshore oil field.

ORCOMBE DESERT ROCKS
The red cliffs along the shoreline around Exmouth belong to the Exmouth Mudstone and Sandstone Formation, laid down in the early Triassic. Prominent headlands like Orcombe Point are formed of sandstone, while sea erosion has carved bays out of the softer mudstone.

BUDLEIGH SALTERTON PEBBLE WALL
This man made wall incorporates pebbles found throughout the area as well as in the cliffs to the west. The cobbles in the Budleigh Salterton Pebble Beds were matched to a rock found in Normandy and Brittany, laid down some 200 million years before they were embedded in the Triassic sandstone. According to Tudor travel writer John Leland, Budleigh's fifteenth-century harbour was "of sum Estimation"; but by the time he arrived in 1540 it was "clene barred" by pebbles washed eastwards to block the mouth of the River Otter. A channel was cleared so that the estuary was navigable to 60-ton vessels until the early nineteenth century; but the Great Hurricane of 1824 drove a spit of pebbles across it, blocking it again.

Littleham Cove's Triassic rocks feature "reduction spots" containing rare metallic elements, including radioactive uranium and vanadium and native silver, as well as minerals derived from a number of other elements. The cause of reduction spots is not known, but it is thought that they result from the presence of microbes when the sediment was being buried. The radiation from these nodules is low-level, but handling them is not recommended.

A little later in the period, the Budleigh Salterton Pebble Beds were swept in by a braided desert river rising to the south. The river continued northwards as far as Yorkshire, until subsidence occurred in what later became the English Channel and the river's flow was reversed. Scattered among the hard quartzite pebbles are a few hard black tourmalinite cobbles, probably formed in association with the Dartmoor granite.

Forests of conifers and palm-like cycads began to spread over the land, and new marine species appeared in the warm seas, including a walrus-like reptile known as a placodont and a giant reptile that established itself as king of the sea, found near Ladram Bay in 1990 and named a rhynchosaur. Later – around 225 million years ago – the first dinosaurs made an entrance. The earliest Triassic ones were no bigger than dogs; but by the end of the period some of them were as long as 6m, and mammals were beginning to appear.

Sea levels began to rise once more, and by about 200 million years ago Southern England again lay beneath a warm, shallow sea. Red and green mudstones were laid down, interspersed with thin layers of gypsum and rock salt evaporated from the lakes. There are exposures of Mercia mudstone rocks at Porlock and at Higher Dunscombe, near Branscombe, where there are crystalline veins of gypsum in the cliffs above.

At the end of the period another mass extinction event wiped out some 76-84% of all species, including most mammal-like reptiles, large amphibians and dinosaurs.

OTTER SANDSTONE BEDDING PLANES

Laid down after the Pebble Beds, the Otter Sandstone was also formed through river action, settling on a layer of wind-blown sand. Cross-bedding – the way the layers are stacked up in the rock – shows that the rivers were still flowing from south to north in meandering channels of varying speeds. The honeycomb rock visible above the Pebble Beds in Budleigh Salterton's cliffs contains the fossilised roots of Triassic plants known as rhizoconcretions, and other plant fossils and some worm-tubes were found at Orcombe Point. Fossil vertebrates in the sandstone include amphibians and reptiles, and there are fossil fish in the mudstone.

SIDMOUTH CLIFFS

The Sidmouth mudstone in the high cliffs at Salcombe contains radioactive nodules, similar to those at Littleham Cove but formed in association with gypsum, indicating the presence of salt lakes in the arid desert landscape. The salt was drawn to the surface of the Triassic rocks by capillary action during evaporation, and it has been exploited since prehistoric times.

THE JURASSIC PERIOD

200 million years ago Pangea was still drifting north; but it was beginning to break up, as huge eruptions along a rift zone created the sea that would later widen into the Atlantic Ocean. Slowly South West England emerged as dry land. Cornwall and most of Devon remained so throughout the Jurassic period, and any rocks deposited then have been eroded, apart from an outcrop of blue lias immediately west of Lyme Regis, where the dark marine limestones and shales are rich in early Jurassic fossils, especially of marine reptiles, including the dolphin-like dinosaurs known as ichthyosaurs.

The area known today as Dorset made its first appearance in the Jurassic period, as a result of sediments deposited in a range of environments – terrestrial, freshwater and marine. From the oldest rocks at Lyme Regis, on the western side of Dorset, the Jurassic beds slope gently to the east in progressively younger strata, with the most recent being around Swanage, where a sculpture trail at Durlston Castle today illustrates their progression.

OSMINGTON TRACE FOSSILS

Osmington beach is one of Britain's most important geological sites, with cliffs and ledges formed from Osmington Oolite. This is composed of "ooliths" (from the Greek "oos", meaning egg) – tiny spheres created from a grain of sand or a fragment of shell being rolled around the bed of a warm, shallow sea and gathering calcium in layers. Many of Osmington's weathered slabs contain trace fossils – the remnants of the burrows and tracks of animals that lived when the rock was being formed. There are also huge boulders, known as "doggers", formed from a sandstone bed which once held large quantities of oil. At Burning Cliff, friction caused by small landslips sometimes ignites the oil remaining between the layers of rock, and an occasional rainbow sheen on the surface of the water indicates the presence of minute quantities washed from the rocks.

Above:

BURTON CLIFF

Around West Bay and Burton Bradstock, the sandstone cliffs are the remains of a large offshore sand bank that advanced southwards in the early part of the Jurassic period, about 175 million years ago. Some of the strata are more resistant to erosion, probably as a result of a calcium carbonate cement formed when stormy seas washed in organic material such as seashells, and the cliffs are topped with younger oolitic limestone.

Right:

MUPE ROCKS

The youngest Jurassic rocks are the Purbeck Beds, a series of clays and limestones deposited in a string of lagoons. They form the cliffs at Durlston, and can also be seen on the shoreline around Lulworth and Mupe Bay. They were laid down on top of the Portland group, displayed in the dramatic limestone-topped cliffs around Portland Bill and St Albans Head. These older rocks were deposited in a shallow sea, and their fossils include giant ammonites known as Titanites.

FOSSIL FOREST
The "thrombolites" in Lulworth Cove's fossil forest – and in another on Portland – were formed in a cypress swamp on the edge of a Jurassic lagoon stretching from Dorset to France. When rising sea levels drowned the forest, the trees were preserved in the layers of limestone deposited on the seabed. Eventually the trees rotted away, leaving hollow mounds where the mud and algae that had formed around their roots were fossilised.

Marine conditions persisted throughout the period, with repeating cycles of the sea deepening and getting shallower. The oldest lias limestones, between Lyme Regis and Bridport, alternate with layers of clay, and the fossils show many ammonites and marine reptiles. From Lyme Regis to Charmouth the rock strata are sandier as a result of falling sea levels as they were formed.

From Burton Bradstock to the Fleet the rocks all date from the Middle Jurassic. The Great Oolite group laid down on top of these include Fuller's Earth clays, formed in deeper water, as well as Frome Clay and Forest Marble, whose fossils show that they were formed in shallow water that was possibly tidal. Later the sea deepened, and rubbly brown limestones known as Cornbrash were deposited, followed by clays. Between Weymouth and Ringstead, the Corallian rocks contain the fossils of the corals that give them their name, while the ammonites in the rocks from Kimmeridge Bay to St Alban's Head show that these were formed in open water that was deeper.

The warm tropical seas teemed with life throughout the period, and the cliffs between Lyme Regis and Charmouth are an internationally important source of Jurassic fossils. It was here that Mary Anning famously found the first ichthyosaur in 1810, the "sea dragon" plesiosaur in 1823, and the "flying-dragon" pterodactyl in 1828. A more recent find was the 3m skeleton of a scelidosaur, a species unique to this area.

THE CRETACEOUS PERIOD

At the start of the Cretaceous period, around 145 million years ago, the Earth was still warm, with no ice at the poles. Sea levels were at their highest ever, and most of southern England was underwater as the Atlantic opened up. The thick beds of mudstones and sandstones formed in lakes and rivers in eastern Dorset were followed by marine sandstones and clays. Once Dorset was completely underwater, the Cinder Bed was formed, mainly of oysters, with marine limestones laid down on top of these, and then freshwater limestones as the sea receded once more. Around Swanage, delta deposits of material were swept from the landmass to the west, with layers of clay and greensand later deposited on top as marine conditions returned.

Much of Devon was underwater, too, although Dartmoor was probably an island. Clays, greensand and chalk were laid down on the eastern side of the county, with marine fossils similar to those in Dorset. Chalk formed in this period consists of the fragmented hard remains of microscopic plankton, known as coccoliths. Flint and clay were formed above.

OLD HARRY ROCKS

As the sea deepened later in the Cretaceous period, the sand contained higher levels of calcium carbonate, forming chalk, with fossils featuring seabed animals. This constitutes the central ridge of inland Dorset and the Purbeck Hills, as well as various outcrops around the coastline and the Old Harry Rocks. In summer the chalk grasslands topping the high cliffs are bright with wildflowers, including the rare early spider orchid.

Dinosaurs dominated in the warm, tropical conditions, leaving fossil footprints in the Purbeck Beds. Top predators in the sea were ichthyosaurs and sea crocodiles; while on land the first flowering plants grew, attracting the very first bees.

HOOKEN CLIFFS AT BEER

Just west of Beer the soaring white cliffs have slumped, leaving a terraced landscape that is a haven for wildlife, like the Undercliffs between Axmouth and Lyme Regis. This part of the coastline is especially prone to landslips, because rainwater easily passes through the porous top strata of chalk and greensand, but cannot drain away through the clays below. Instead it spreads sideways, acting as a lubricant between the layers; and since the underlying rocks are tilted towards the sea, finally the top rocks slide into the sea.

Sometime in 1788, the stream running across the common at the top of Hooken Cliffs became blocked underground, and the water pooled on top of the clays. Within a year a fissure behind the clifftop separated about 10 acres from the land beyond. One night in March 1790, this portion of the cliff finally pulled away, releasing 15 million tons of chalk and greensand on to the beach nearly 100m below. The ridge that formed on the seabed as a result moved the shoreline about 200m out to sea, and the next morning, crab pots that had been laid several metres below sea level were found 5m above it.

THE TERTIARY PERIOD

65 million years ago another disastrous mass extinction event wiped out all the dinosaurs and many flowering plants. There are many theories about the origins of this disaster; but it is known that its grand finale was when a huge asteroid or comet landed on the Mexican seabed. The extinction of the dinosaurs and giant reptiles now gave other species a chance. Mammals and birds were able to flourish for the first time, and from here the evolution of these species proceeded at a great rate.

At the beginning of the Tertiary period the temperature rose, and sea levels with it. The climate became wetter, and dense tropical and subtropical forests spread across the land. As global warming progressed there were even forests at the poles. Britain had a climate similar to today's Asian subtropics, although it was still drifting northwards and slowly cooling, and southern England was still under a shallow sea.

Slowly more of the British Isles became land, and the opening of the Atlantic Ocean began to affect its climate and so the evolution of its lifeforms. Fossils laid down in Dorset and East Devon show that many of the species dominating the landscape were plants and animals that we would recognise today.

DORSET WETLANDS

Around Poole, the thick clays of the Poole Formation and the chalk basin underlying deposits of gravel, sands and silts have given rise to well-drained acidic soils. The Dorset Heaths Natural Area is one of the country's most important wildlife sites, with a mix of habitats including wetlands, heathland, fens and woodlands. Nightjars and woodlarks flourish in the coniferous plantations, while the older woodlands provide a home for many species of moths and butterflies, and rare lichens. The open heathland is home to many unusual insects, including three species of spider not found anywhere else in Britain. All six species of British reptile flourish here, and there are frogs, toads and newts in the bogs, with 28 different dragonfly species hovering above.

STAIR HOLE

The famous "Lulworth Crumple" at Stair Hole was a result of vertical strata of shale collapsing under their own weight, leaving bands of harder limestone sagging together. Ranging from 150-60 million years old, the rocks at Lulworth Cove were formed underwater and later tilted by Earth movements. After the last Ice Age, an enormous river of glacial meltwater carved itself a passage through the rock to the coast, allowing the sea to flood in. The waves eroded the softer rocks behind the hard headland of Portland limestone, creating the iconic cove. Later, they carved the cliffs into arches and then stacks.

Gradually the climate became cooler and drier, and glaciers appeared. The forests began to diminish, especially the tropical ones, and grasslands took over as many new species of grass evolved and prairie animals roamed the new plains. Subsidence in Devon led to thick accumulations of sediments, resulting in the formation of an enormous lake, fed from water cascading off the Dartmoor mountains. Huge volumes of sand and mud were washed into the basin, along with plant debris. Later kelp forests began to appear.

India was still drifting north and as it collided with the Eurasian continent, the Himalayas were raised. Africa was an island at this point, and not yet attached to Europe or the Middle East. Its own journey northwards and its subsequent collision with the continental landmass caused the Alps to form, around 20 million years ago. Dorset's rocks were folded during this orogeny, creating the series of ridges seen through the county today.

With the uplifting of the landmass following the Alpine orogeny, Britain was now almost completely land, with some tidal coastal plains and shallow sea across parts of southern and eastern England. With the continent still heading north, the climate was cooling and glacial conditions setting in. No longer underwater, Devon's surface rocks were now exposed to weathering and the chalk layers were worn away, leaving areas of flint gravel in the east. The large lake was still filling with clays, sands, gravels and brown coals, spread along the Sticklepath Fault line, which runs across the county from Bideford Bay to Torquay, where it can be seen in the cliff face at Rock Walk.

THE ICE AGES

Around five million years ago, apes began to separate out into chimps and the first humans, and there was ice at the north and south poles, fluctuating with the seasons. After about three million years global temperatures fell again, and today's ice cap formed on the North Pole. Everywhere else was given over to grassland and tundra, although Cornwall was still under a shallow sea, where beds of sand and clay were deposited. At St Erth, Mediterranean marine fossils were found some 30m above today's sea level, with a number of layers of

GIANTS QUOITS

During the cold, dry intervals of the Ice Age, dust clouds deposited a fine silt known as loess in various locations around Cornwall. At Dean Point the loess is 2m deep in places, providing rich nutrients for plants. Combined with the mild climate and the local gabbro – itself a source of fertile soil – this has resulted in a unique habitat, supporting many nationally rare species of plants , notably the Cornish heath (Erica Vagans) which only occurs in a single location outside the Lizard peninsula. The natural formation known as Giant's Quoits once stood on Dean Point, but it was moved to its present position above Porthoustock to safeguard it from the quarrying activities below.

SAUNTON PINK GRANITE
Saunton Sands beach is noted for the glacial erratics on its raised beach platform, including one massive boulder of pink granite, matched to rocks on Gruinard Bay. These boulders – swept from North West Scotland – show that the glacier melt reached this far, even though the ice sheets did not. A couple of miles from Saunton, deposits brought in the same way led to a particularly fertile soil on Braunton's Great Field; and across the estuary, Fremington's fine pottery clays were formed from till, or boulder clay, carried in by the ice sheets.

PORTLAND BILL RAISED BEACH
At Portland Bill, there are two distinct levels of platform cut into the limestone, showing completely different sea levels. When ice caps formed during the cold snaps, water was locked into the ice and sea levels dropped. Meltwater during the warmer intervals raised them again; only for them to drop once more as the land, relieved of the weight of all that ice, rose a little. A marine abrasion platform is visible around much of Devon and Cornwall, cut by the waves when sea levels were higher.

different sedimentary deposits beneath them, including a band of quartz pebbles swept from older rocks.

Since the start of the current Ice Age there have been at least twenty cycles of freezing and thawing, with glaciers advancing and retreating and sea levels fluctuating accordingly. During the cold intervals, global temperatures were 5 degrees lower than today's and the climate was much drier, because the moisture was locked into the ice sheets. Rainfall in Europe was about half its current level, and in places the winter temperatures were as much as 20 degrees colder. Deserts expanded and the ice sheets ground rocks to dust, so that there were frequent dust storms whipped up by the higher wind speeds.

Only three or four of the glacial periods produced ice sheets in Britain, and none of these reached South West England. The sea level was up to 120m lower than today's, and the English Channel and the North Sea were both dry land. In Dorset, tundra conditions shaped the chalk downs and large quantities of gravel were swept around Poole by the Solent River, before later sea level rises flooded the area.

VALLEY OF ROCKS

As well as raised beach deposits and high sea cliffs, another relic of the fluctuating temperatures is the debris of ice-shattered rocks lying in valleys and on the slopes above them. This process of freeze and thaw also led to dry valleys, with deposits of weathered material swept into the valleys by the ice melt. North Devon's Valley of Rocks is a particularly spectacular example of this, with its weathered crags towering over a valley where there is no river.

2
THE PREHISTORIC LANDSCAPE

THE PALAEOLITHIC PERIOD

DURING THE WARM intervals of the Ice Age, the climate was similar to today's. Mammoths' teeth have been found in the River Sid, and the coastline from the Exe to Lyme Regis has produced the tusks, bones and teeth of elephant and rhinoceros. At Porlock, a fragment of a stone handaxe tentatively dated at around 300,000 years old shows that there were Stone Age toolmakers hunting these animals on the South West coastline in the Lower Palaeolithic (Early Stone Age) period. On the Somerset shoreline, sediments show the fossils of reindeer, bison, Arctic foxes and lemmings from a cooler period 50,000 years ago, and the bones and tusks of woolly mammoths.

The last major Ice Age began around 30,000 years ago. Britain was still joined to mainland Europe, and during the warm intervals the earliest human inhabitants roamed freely along the southern edge of the ice sheets, around the upper reaches of the River Severn. These first people were hunters, a migrant population following the herds of wild animals. As the temperature fluctuated, the ice sheet advanced and retreated, and with it the animals and their followers. At its coldest, between 18,000 and 11,500 years ago, the British climate was too harsh for human settlement and the hunters withdrew temporarily south until the temperature rose again.

THE MESOLITHIC PERIOD

As rising temperatures marked the end of this cold snap, the frozen landscape in South West England gave way to mixed woodland – birches and willows, followed by Scots pines and oaks. On the higher ground, peat bogs began to form. Sea levels rose as the ice melted, and the kinder climate encouraged the hunters to linger in small groups around the coastline, fishing and collecting shellfish. During this Mesolithic (Middle Stone Age) period, they were able to catch smaller mammals and birds, and plants flourished in the warmer environment, providing nuts and berries as a new source of food.

Opposite:
BEER FLINT WALL
Beer was the region's best flint source for Stone Age man's tools and weapons. Formed in association with the Cretaceous chalk, the steely properties that make it a good building stone were accompanied by its propensity to split into sharp flakes when struck, and numerous scatters of Palaeolithic flint flakes have been found on the high ground around Beer, and around Studland and Swanage, where a Palaeolithic stone axe was also discovered. There were more on Northam Burrows and in the Bude area. At Praa Sands, Palaeolithic hearths with burnt bones were found. Godrevy was a hotspot for Britain's prehistoric population, with flint tools dating from the Upper Palaeolithic, when the ice sheets were just beginning to melt for the last time before the present warm interlude.

Portland's Culverwell is one of the first ever human settlements on mainland Britain, and a pierced scallop shell and a pebble were found flanking a polished axe head beneath a large triangular stone, thought to have been a memorial, showing that even these early people had a sense of spirituality. Culverwell's Mesolithic population laid stone slabs laid over a seashell midden – the first known use of Portland stone for building purposes – and archaeologists dated the charcoal and molluscs on their hearth to around 6000BC.

New tools were needed now, for fishing and snaring small land animals, and the flint tools from this period were smaller, broad-blade "microliths", used for the tips of wooden arrows and spears. Later these were mounted in series on wooden shafts to make saw-tooth blades.

Large scatters of Mesolithic tools were found on Thorncombe Beacon, at Corfe Castle and Kimmeridge, and at Hope Cove. There was a flint-working site on Northam Burrows, probably the source of the tools and arrowheads found on the Taw. There were Mesolithic settlements in Godrevy and around Marazion, and scatterings of flint tools were found right around Cornwall's coastline. In Holywell, archaeologists unearthed a shell and bone midden; and flint axe-heads and scrapers found near Minehead were dated at 12,000 years old. Flint tools were found at Selworthy Beacon and around Countisbury, with a particular concentration around Porlock, where a flint-working site was identified at Hawkridge. Archaeologists believe that this was the summer hunting camp of a small band of family groups who dropped to the lower ground in winter.

Sea levels continued rising throughout the period, and sometime around 8000 years ago the Atlantic Ocean and the North Sea flowed right through the low areas surrounding Britain, forming the English Channel and finally isolating Britain from the rest of Europe. Gradually the forest that stretched from Minehead to Wales was drowned by the ever-widening River Severn, which eventually became the Bristol Channel, turning South West England into a peninsula. Fossilised tree stumps and peat beds can be seen in the shingle at low tide at Porlock Weir and Warren Point, and fossilised pollens and seeds show that 6000 years ago Porlock Bay was a salt marsh, surrounded by reeds and alders.

On many South West beaches, a combination of particularly low tides and stormy weather still reveals the fossilised remains of this drowned wildwood. In Mount's Bay, severe storms in 2013/4 laid bare a substantial area of the forest which once surrounded St Michael's Mount, and at Penzance, fossilised tree trunks 5m long were identified as oak and pine, with the remnants of hazel thickets exposed among them. At Daymer Bay, the same storms exposed fossil soils containing snails that are now extinct and the shell middens

PORLOCK SHINGLE

At Porlock in October 1996, huge storm waves generated by Hurricane Lillie and amplified by an unusually high tide drove through the shingle ridge, demolishing it further as they swept back out to sea. As well as exposing the remnants of Porlock Weir's submarine forest it dredged up the fossilised bones of the famous Porlock Aurochs, a large ox estimated to be around 3500 years old.

It was the last straw for Porlock. A century and a half of intensive restructuring of the shingle barrier had done nothing but make things worse, and the decision was made to stop trying to keep the sea out and let nature take its course. Less than a decade later, under the watchful gaze of international experts, it turned out to be the right thing to do. The waves washed the shingle into a stable barrier and a saltmarsh developed in the low-lying ground behind, home to a wide range of birds, unusual plants and some nationally rare lichens.

of the area's dense Mesolithic population. Portmellon Cove's submerged forest contained fossils of alder, birch, hazel and oak, with bogbean and white waterlily seeds showing that they fringed a pool or lake. Beech, willow, elm, ash and holly once flourished at Millendreath Beach, and yellow iris shows that this was marshland.

CHESIL TOMBOLO

Rising sea levels after the last Ice Age swept seabed sediments into what later became the 18-mile shingle barrier of Chesil Beach. During this process the shingle ridge was driven inland, forming the beach 7000-5000 years ago. It started out sandy, with layers of shell and coarser materials deposited on top; but as rising sea levels battered the East Devon cliffs, much bigger boulders were dislodged and washed on to the barrier ridge by longshore drift. Behind it, the Fleet Lagoon is still joined to the sea by a narrow channel at Portland Harbour. Seawater percolating through the shingle mixes with freshwater washed down from the hills, giving a wide range of salt levels and temperatures and creating an unusual habitat for no fewer than 150 different species of seaweed. This provides food for many molluscs and fish, themselves a larder for the great flocks of seabirds to be seen on The Fleet throughout the year. Resident species include large numbers of swans, geese, ducks, herons and egrets, and many other wildfowl. Land species include pheasants, quails and partridges, as well as migrant birds of prey such as harriers, hobbies and even red kites.

As sea levels rose, erosion carved out coves and then bays. The waves swept away the rocks that fell into the sea, driving them vast distances along the coastline in the process known as longshore drift, turning them into rounded boulders and then pebbles that fetched up on the peninsula's shingle beaches. The most dramatic of these is Dorset's famous Chesil Beach, linking Portland to the mainland in a dramatic tombolo, where the mix of seawater and freshwater through the shingle has created a rare habitat in the Fleet Lagoon behind it. Other shingle beaches formed at Porlock, Westward Ho!, Loe Bar and Slapton Sands, backed by lagoons or marshland providing rare habitats for unusual species.

SWANPOOL WILLOW CARR

At Falmouth's Swanpool, a nineteenth-century culvert constructed to drain freshwater from a natural lake into the sea resulted in an artificial lagoon that supports a large number of species, including Britain's only Trembling Sea Mat. This underwater reef is composed of billions of primitive microscopic organisms living in colonies attached to stones or the stems of plants and feeding on particles trapped using hairy tentacles. In the marshland behind the lagoon, a densely wooded wetland of mostly willow carr acts as a natural filter, removing pollutants from the six streams and providing shelter and food for birds and small mammals. Willow can support as many as 450 different species of invertebrate, and over 100 different species of bird have been spotted here. Many rushes, ferns, mosses and lichens flourish in the moist conditions.

CARRICK ROADS

In Falmouth itself, this post-Ice Age flooding drowned the mouth of the river valley, turning Carrick Roads into one of the world's best natural deep-water harbours. Other drowned river valleys – "rias" – include Poole Harbour, Plymouth Sound and the Erme and Avon estuaries, and the waterways at Dartmouth, Exmouth, Helford, Fowey and Salcombe. Their wildlife ranges from large mammals such as dolphins, porpoises, basking sharks and seals to rare underwater plants like eelgrass, Britain's only marine flowering plant and a valuable habitat for sea slugs, cuttlefish, seahorses and young bass. Oysters are farmed in the Helford Estuary, and Falmouth boasts Europe's last commercial fleet working purely under sail, the consequence of an 1868 bye-law prohibiting oyster-dredging by any mechanically-propelled craft.

PORTHKIDNEY HABITAT

On the Atlantic coast, large quantities of sand were blown into the Hayle estuary, and Porthkidney Sands are backed by a large area of dunes. Formed from crushed seashells, the sand is rich in lime and supports an unusual array of wildflowers, including Mountain St John's wort and the Hebridean orchid. The UK's most southwesterly estuary, the Hayle rarely freezes, making it an important site for overwintering birds. As many as 18,000 birds flock here in a cold winter.

Between the River Hayle and the headland at Godrevy, the Towans (Cornish for "dunes") are Cornwall's second-largest dune system. Facing north west, they are exposed to the full force of Atlantic storms and the sand is continually shifting, scouring the surface bare along the shoreline. The sea stacks are still topped by the remnants of dunes, making them of particular importance to geologists. Later agricultural and industrial use of this area has resulted in additional habitats, and a third of all plant species found in Cornwall can be seen here, attracting rare butterflies and moths.

DAWLISH WARREN INVERTEBRATES

Towards the tidal limit of the estuaries and creeks, the sandbanks give way to mudflats, where large numbers of invertebrates live – a larder packed with nutrients for hungry birds! Up to 20,000 waterbirds feed and roost along the Exe Estuary, home to large flocks of Brent geese and black-tailed godwits, and its avocets form one of Britain's largest flocks. Dawlish Warren's mudflats are a particularly valuable environment for migrant birds looking for somewhere to rest during their epic journey. Between September and April, as many as 8,000 wading birds can be seen roosting here at high tide. The site also supports over 600 species of plants, including a very rare liverwort and the sand crocus, found in only one other location in the UK.

PENHALE DUNES

Other north-coast rias swamped by sand are the Taw and Torridge, the Camel and the Gannel. At Penhale, Cornwall's largest dune system (and Britain's highest) covers 650 hectares at 90m above sea level and was formed when changing sea levels caused sand to accumulate on a rocky plateau. Strong onshore winds drive large quantities of sand on to the higher ground behind the dunes, providing a habitat for unusual communities of plants and insects. As the sand travels inland, it leaves behind areas that have been eroded to the water table, resulting in marshy ground whose species include scented meadowsweet and water mint and rare butterflies like the grizzled skipper, found in only two colonies in Cornwall.

SAUNTON DUNE

The 1350-hectare dune system at Braunton Burrows, the focus of North Devon's UNESCO Biosphere Reserve, is internationally known for its wildlife. Some of its dunes are 30m high, and over 400 different plant species have been recorded here, many of them rare. Across the estuary, "the surges of the bay have defeated their own fury, by rolling up in the course of ages a rampart of grey boulder stones," according to Charles Kingsley's novel "Westward Ho!" Kingsley went on to describe how the shingle barrier "protects from the high tides of spring and autumn a fertile sheet of smooth alluvial turf." Overwintering and migratory birds gather on Northam Burrows, and a number of rare plants flourish in the unusual habitat. From medieval days, local residents wealthy enough to possess two hearths were entitled to common grazing rights on Northam Burrows. In return, during an annual ceremony known as "potwalloping", they were expected to gather up and replace the cobbles that had been swept from the ridge by spring tides, to prevent the sea from breaching the bank.

THE NEOLITHIC PERIOD

With the continental land bridges gone, Britain's prehistoric population had to settle down. Neolithic (Late Stone Age) man set about clearing areas of the woodland to make hunting easier. It was the beginning of the end for the wildwood, and today its last remnants can only be seen on hillsides too steep for the trees to have been felled, as in Lee's Borough Wood. Near Crackington Haven, parts of Trebarfoote Wood are designated "ancient woodland" – the original wildwood – with areas of "ancient semi-natural woodland", where trees have been preserved through coppicing, as they have in Looe's Kilminorth Wood and many other places.

COASTAL WOODLAND

On the steep scree-clad coastal slopes between Clovelly and Porlock, Britain's longest stretch of coastal woodland survives the buffeting of the salt-laden air, thanks largely to the shelter provided by its tall cliffs. Known as Atlantic Oakwoods, Britain's "temperate rainforest" consists largely of the hardy trees which took root first after the Ice Age – sessile oak, Scots pine, downy birch and rowan, with a hazel and holly understorey. The clean, moist coastal air provides a damp microclimate resulting in lush vegetation, with extensive areas of ferns, mosses and lichens and two species of whitebeam not found anywhere else in the UK.

MUTTER'S MOOR

Many of the UK's heathlands result from the Neolithic clearance of the wildwood. During the Bronze and Iron Ages, prehistoric farmers burnt areas of scrub to produce fresh grazing. Eventually this destroyed the soil, leaving an acid, freely-draining surface of low fertility where bracken and heather flourish, producing heathland. On Mutter's Moor, above Sidmouth, succeeding generations cut turves from the peat and used the scrub and bracken for fuel and animal bedding, depleting the vegetation and soil nutrients further.

WEST PENWITH FIELDS
Neolithic farmers enclosed small fields around their scattered settlements, using earthen banks or stone hedges, adding further fields piecemeal. The rough ground beyond was common grazing. In West Penwith these tiny patchwork fields are the world's oldest structures still in use.

The Neolithic people came by boat, bringing many new skills. They cultivated wheat, oats and barley, and brought sheep, horses, goats, cattle, chickens. They made cloth from linen and wool, and their pottery has been found at Gwithian and Porthscatho in Cornwall and on Mutter's Moor in Devon, where their flint tools have been discovered too, as they have at Hooken Cliffs and Gwennap Head.

Where flint was not locally available they used greenstone. This was quarried at Trenow, near Marazion, and there was an axe factory here too. Tools were also manufactured at Cape Cornwall, St Ives and Mousehole. A greenstone axe was found at Cawsand, and others were discovered on Exmoor, as well as greenstone arrowheads. There was a lively trade in these tools and weapons, at home and abroad. Neolithic tools were finely chiselled and highly polished, and at Gwithian they were found to have reworked crude Mesolithic tools using their own refined techniques.

ZENNOR QUOIT
The high heathland of West Penwith is also the location for some of the most remarkable Neolithic monuments, like the Zennor Quoit. These early tombs, as well as places to bury the dead, served as territory markers with elaborate rituals designed to bond the population with their land. Two or three generations were entombed in a communal grave before the entrance was sealed.

TREGESEAL HOLED STONE
Near Cape Cornwall, the Tregeseal stone circle is thought to have been part of a ritual complex of two or three such circles, and a number of holed stones nearby are thought to be associated with it, although their function is not known. Legend has it that the Merry Maidens circle, near St Buryan, was formed when the Devil turned some young maidens to stone for dancing on a Sunday. Exmoor's Culbone stone row dates from around this time, as did the Seven Stones circle that stood on Mutter's Moor near Sidmouth before it was removed to a local garden.

THE BRONZE AGE

Sometime around 2000BC, the "Beaker People" arrived, although it is thought that the beakers may have arrived before them, in the trade that was happening between Britain and the continent. In 1896 one of these beakers was found beside the skeleton in a Bronze Age cist on Yenworthy Common, Exmoor. Other items found in Bronze Age graves include buttons made from jet and shale and arrowheads of a much more sophisticated design than previous weapons, and numerous artefacts showing that metalworking skills had arrived in Britain for the first time.

BURGH ISLAND
At the mouth of the Erme, near Mary's Rocks – notorious for their shipwrecks – divers found the remains of a Bronze Age tin-trader's vessel, carrying rough ingots made by melting tin in earth moulds. Thought to be cast on Dartmoor around 1000BC, they showed that Burgh Island was an international tin-trading centre. Other important Bronze Age trade centres included Portland, St Michael's Mount and Plymouth's Mount Batten.

By now, tin streaming was being carried out in Cornwall. This process of extracting tin from running water continued until medieval times, and can still be seen in operation at the Blue Hills tin mine near St Agnes. Many centuries later, the same operation was used to salvage tin that had been lost from dressing floors in mines, and remnants of this industrial process are preserved in Hayle's Red River Valley Nature Reserve.

Irish toolmakers had already been producing copper arrowheads toughened with an arsenic compound (arsenic occurs naturally in copper reserves and was later extracted in tandem with the copper). Now some smart metalworker discovered that tin added to copper produced bronze, a hard shiny alloy that was both practical and pretty, and suddenly Cornish tin was in global demand. A simultaneous gold rush in Ireland made Cornwall a key location on a trade route that linked Ireland and mainland Britain with the rest of Europe and other Mediterranean countries. Two Bronze Age hoards of Irish gold were found beside this ancient trade route, on holloways in West Penwith. One, discovered by quarryworkers near Morvah in 1884, consisted of six large bracelets; the other was found in a Bronze Age stone hedge in 1931 and included rods, neckrings and armbands, all made of Irish gold.

In Harlyn Bay, necklaces of amber and blue glass beads from the Mediterranean were found in a complex multi-period prehistoric cemetery of over 100 graves, and a Bronze Age dagger found in a grave in Pelynt originated in the Aegean.

These Bronze Age settlers lived in small hamlets of round huts, linked by protective walls or built within an enclosure, and they too were farmers. In Gwithian, ancient plough marks have been dated to the Bronze Age. Penwith's Bronze Age population adapted the Neolithic field system to their own form of agriculture, with small fields intensively cultivated, using terraced banks known as strip lynchets. The heathland was still common grazing, and the arable land was divided fairly to give everyone some good ground – a democratic system that continued through medieval times and can still be seen at Bosigran and Predannack Wollas.

By the end of the Bronze Age, most of the ancient wildwood had been cleared and was replaced by new woodland, managed for its timber by means of coppicing. Farmers started rotating crops, and animal husbandry intensified, with ever-lengthening tracks to the common land beyond. Cattle were raised in the more fertile pastureland on the lower ground, while sure-footed sheep reared in the uplands during the summer were brought to lower ground in the autumn.

TREVELGUE HEAD

There were hut circles and a bronze foundry on Trevelgue Head, one of the South West's chief settlements when Cornwall's trade routes ran inland from north to south. Early sea traders avoided the treacherous waters around Land's End and the Lizard by travelling overland to the opposite coast and continuing their sea journey from there. Later these routes were used by pilgrims on their way to Christian sites such as north-western Spain's Cathedral of St James in Santiago de Compostela. Two of these ancient pathways exist as leisure walking routes today: St Michael's Way, running from Lelant to St Michael's Mount; and the Forth an Syns (The Saints Way), connecting Padstow with Fowey.

Archaeologists excavating Bronze Age barrows often find skeletons with their knees drawn up. Cornwall's Constantine Island made headlines in 2008, when an amateur archaeologist found the remains of a middle-aged Bronze Age man buried in this position. Later in the period, cremations were commonplace, and cremated bones were discovered in a barrow recently excavated at Godrevy Head. Charcoal was found beneath the cairn rubble in three burial mounds at Golden Cap, Dorset.

HEAVEN'S GATE

The size and site of the Heaven's Gate barrow, high above Kimmeridge Bay, reflects the status of its occupant. There was the beginning of a social hierarchy in the Bronze Age, and people buried their dead in individual mounds generally no more than a couple of metres high. In Osmington, Goggin's Barrow is at the foot of the South Dorset Ridgeway, where there are many other Bronze Age barrows, and the remains of strip lynchets. A large round barrow on Perranporth's Cubert Common is believed to have been a particularly important burial site, and there are numerous Bronze Age mounds and cairns in the heather around Selworthy Beacon. Smaller Bronze Age barrows can be seen right around the coastline.

BALLOWALL BARROW

Cornish antiquary W.C. Borlase discovered Ballowall Barrow under a mound of mining debris near his home in Pendeen. Excavating it, he found five small stone-lined cists containing pottery, thought to have been Bronze Age cremation urns. Two pits within the same mound were possibly graves, and there is a Neolithic "entrance grave" beneath the surrounding apron.

THE IRON AGE

Around 3000 years ago the British climate became colder and wetter. The water table rose, and so did the sea. On the higher ground, peat and blanket bog began to spread, while below it heathland took over. The population was on the increase, too, with something like a quarter of a million people on mainland Britain. Wholesale land clearance and intensive farming began to put pressure on the amount of arable land available; and these peaceful, pastoral people found they needed to defend their territories for the first time in history.

Sometime after 500BC, the Iron Age began as the Celts arrived – brawny, belligerent people with slashing weapons made of a much sturdier metal than bronze. They defended the lands they claimed by building earth and stone banks around strategic high spots. On the coast, they constructed ramparts across the necks of headlands already protected on three sides by high seacliffs. In Cornwall there were almost as many promontory forts as there are headlands. Often the headland's later name included some variation on the word "din" or "dinas" (Cornish for "fort"), as in Trereen Dinas and Pendennis.

One of the earliest cliff castles was at Sennen Cove, where a simple stone bank across the headland protected a cluster of round houses. Trevelgue Head's seven or eight ramparts, enclosing a large settlement and its field system, was built primarily to protect the iron ore in Black Humphrey's Rock and the associated smelting works. Other particularly significant Cornish promontory forts are at Gurnard's Head, the Rumps and Tintagel Island. In Dorset, much of the Flowers Barrow has been lost to the sea, but archaeologists found traces of cross dykes nearby, with strip lynchets up to ten feet high cut into the hillside.

The cliff castle at Embury Beacon was refortified later, more than once, and archaeologists found sling stones here. Iron Age pottery was dated to around 200BC, and spindle whorls and whetstones showed evidence of spinning and metalwork. At the Rumps, parts of an oak and hazel loom indicate that they also wove cloth. Other Iron Age goods found in the region include ores of iron, tin and copper, obtained from surface mining, and moulds, ingots and crucibles used in smelting. As well as iron tools and weapons, ornate bronze artefacts have been discovered, often elaborately decorated with glass and enamel.

The multi-period cemetery in Harlyn Bay included Iron Age skeletons, buried in slate coffins with their skulls fractured (thought to let their souls escape). Another Iron Age cemetery was found at Trelan Bahow near St Keverne, where the artefacts buried with the bodies were more elaborate, and finds included an engraved bronze hand mirror, showing that now women, too, had sufficient status to merit personal wealth in the afterlife.

DODMAN POINT BULWARK
The double ramparts of one of Cornwall's most spectacular promontory forts still cross the neck of Dodman Point. In places both banks of the bulwark were as high as 2m above the ditch between them, and overall it was 900m long, enclosing 50 acres of land. A Napoleonic signal house stands within it, and an enormous granite cross, erected in 1896 as a navigation aid after two naval destroyers collided.

BOLT TAIL PROMONTORY FORT

Massive ramparts completely enclosed the high headland at Bolt Tail in Devon, affording its defenders strategic views across Hope Cove, where 1500 years later the Spanish Armada was put to flight. Across the county, near Lynton, Countisbury Castle made use of the natural defences of the plunging hillside of the East Lyn Gorge as well as the high seacliffs – an excellent defensive location which the Saxons later used to their advantage against the Vikings.

POOLE HARBOUR

Mount Batten, Plymouth, was still a key port in the Iron Age, as was Hengistbury Head, near Poole. Around 250-200BC a timber mole was constructed in Poole Harbour, allowing ships to draw up in the sheltered waters beside it. Exports included Kimmeridge shale, salt, iron, silver, lead, tin and copper. The Greek geographer Strabo added to this list hides, corn, hunting dogs and slaves.

There is also evidence of continuing trade, at home and abroad. The Greek explorer Pytheas of Massalia noted a flourishing tin trade in Cornwall when he visited Britain in 325BC, and at Gunwalloe archaeologists found an Iron Age shale bracelet from Kimmeridge and pieces of a clay amphora from the Mediterranean. In Falmouth harbour, a 72kg Iron Age tin ingot was dredged up, believed to be destined for the Mediterranean. Spindle whorls and bone combs found at Bantham Ham show that trading partners included the Phoenicians.

CHYSAUSTER

West Penwith's rich archaeological heritage includes settlements of oval stone-walled houses, built around AD25 but still in occupation several centuries later. Each of these "courtyard houses" has several rooms opening on to a central courtyard. At Chysauster – the best-known of the area's 40-odd Iron Age settlements – there were eight of these houses on either side of a street, facing away from the prevailing winds. Each had a living room, a workshop, a stable and a small garden. Stone-lined conduits provided a water supply, and beyond the village there were terraced fields.

Away from the coast, Iron Age people lived in fortified enclosures on hillslopes, still with strategic views over the surrounding land but with less emphasis on defence. Good examples can be seen at Gear and Caervallack, above the Helford River. The earthen banks around these enclosures probably simply contained and sheltered animals. Some of the more dramatic hillforts were the headquarters of tribal chieftains keen to display their social standing; but others show little evidence of dwellings inside their earthworks, and may have been used for ritual or trade purposes, or simply for community gatherings. Elsewhere the earthworks and stone banks surrounded large clusters of round houses.

At Trenow, the remnants of round houses have a prehistoric field system around them, and setts where iron was worked. Iron Age hut circles, some with field systems, can still be seen at Ballard Down, East Portlemouth, Boswinger, Bosigran, Willapark and Forrabury.

CARN EUNY FOGOU
An unusual Iron Age feature is the underground chamber known as a fogou (from a Cornish word meaning "cave", and believed to be unique to Cornwall). Some experts believe that they may have been used for religious rites, while others think they were used for storage or as a hideout. Archaeologists dated pottery found in the Carn Euny fogou to AD118.

3
INTO THE DARK AGES

THE ROMANS

ABBOTSBURY CASTLE IRON AGE hillfort, occupied by the Durotriges tribe, had far-reaching views over the Dorset coastline, making it ideally placed to resist cross-Channel invaders when the Romans arrived in AD43; but there were 40,000 troops in the 1000 Romans galleys sent to conquer Britain's southern shores, and Abbotsbury fell almost as soon as they had landed.

Exeter (Isca) became the civic centre for the Dumnonii tribe of Devon and Cornwall, and Dorchester (Durnovaria) for the Durotriges. Marazion was probably the Roman settlement known as Ictis, and Tintagel the military outpost Durocornovium; but other than exploiting the region's mineral resources, Roman activities in the South West were largely confined to Dorset and East Devon and the region's established trading centres. Villas were built at Honeyditches, overlooking the Axe Estuary, and near Uplyme, both founded on Iron Age settlements, and there was a villa in Illogan.

The South West's few substantial Roman finds were from around the coast, in West Penwith, Camborne and Newquay, and in Plymouth and Torquay, with particular concentrations around West Bay, Portland and Purbeck. Kimmeridge and the Swanage area were exploited for their salt, stone, shale and shale oil, while East Devon provided rich pickings in salt and stone. There was extensive quarrying of high-quality building stone in Beer Caves, with a garrison at nearby Bovey to protect them. Later the same quarries provided the stone for 24 cathedrals, including St Paul's, as well as Westminster Abbey, the Tower of London, Hampton Court and Windsor Castle. Blocks weighing as much as four tons were quarried by hand and transported by horse-drawn wagons or in barges launched from Beer beach. Today the massive underground caverns are a world-famous bat hibernaculum, where over 220 bats – representing most of Britain's 17 species – have been spotted sleeping out the winter.

At Ash Hole, near Berry Head, Victorian archaeologists found enormous quantities of animal bones which turned out to be the kitchen midden from a military camp on the site of the Iron Age fort. Broken pottery found beneath the kitchen waste was dated to the

Opposite:
BREA HILL
Poet Laureate John Betjeman was buried in St Enodoc churchyard below the Roman camp on Brea Hill, which overlooks the Camel estuary. A Victorian local found Roman coins in the dunes around the hill, with bronze medals, pottery, glass jars, vases and beads, jewellery, chains, tweezers, and much wood ash and slag.

Roman period, with coins depicting Emperors Claudius and Nero.

On the Exmoor coastline, the Romans set up a camp to keep an eye on the unruly Welsh Silure tribe, siting it at Old Burrow, at County Gate, with splendid views across the Bristol Channel. Around AD50, between 65 and 80 soldiers were stationed here in tents, with an elaborate field oven built into the fort's earthen ramparts. When this proved to be too exposed, the Romans shifted their Bristol Channel HQ to Martinhoe, constructing two timber barrack blocks, a forge and armoury, and several field ovens made of clay and timber. This fortlet enjoyed similarly strategic views across to Wales; but again the price was an inhospitable upland environment, and a number of unfortunate soldiers froze to death.

The region's peasant farmers lived in clusters of huts enclosed by low earth ramparts. Workmen digging at Caerhays – from the Cornish "kari", meaning an enclosed settlement – found a hoard of 2500 Roman coins. In Cornwall alone there are over a thousand of these settlements, known as Romano-British rounds, occupied long after the Romans had left and visible today on the Roseland peninsula.

JORDAN HILL TEMPLE FOUNDATIONS

The foundations of the Jordan Hill Romano-Celtic temple can be seen above the Coast Path at Weymouth's Bowleaze. The fourth-century building had a verandah for open-air ceremonies, and the site was surrounded by a large walled enclosure found to contain animal bones and coins. More than 80 people were buried nearby with personal objects such as pots, jewellery and arrowheads; and a separate hoard of over 4000 bronze coins, found in 1928, is thought to have accumulated from offerings made at the shrine. Beneath the sanctuary wall, archaeologists found a 4m pit lined with slabs, with 16 layers of charcoal and ash alternating with courses of slabs. Beneath each layer – as in the Celtic ritual pits – a small coin was buried with the bones of a bird. In the bottom layer were two urns, a spearhead and a sword.

ST CONSTANTINES WELL
After Constantine moved his HQ from Rome to Constantinople in response to pressure on the empire's eastern flank, recalling his troops from Britain, the Britons elected leaders from among their tribal chieftains. The Dumnonii's own King Constantine reigned from 407 to 411, and his well still stands in the village named after him. Sixth-century chronicler Gildas called him an "unclean whelp", accusing him of disguising himself as a bishop to murder his two young nephews in a church. As Constantine was chasing a deer, it blundered into the tiny cell of local hermit St Petroc. Deeply impressed by the man's holiness, Constantine renounced his evil ways and was baptised. Abdicating his throne in favour of his son, he founded churches in Falmouth and Illogan, and his mother, Helen, established an oratory at Cape Cornwall, on a site marked today by a crumbling cowshed.

Christianity had reached Cornwall by now, thanks to its trade links with the Mediterranean. Christ is said to have visited Looe himself as a teenager, accompanying his great-uncle, Phoenician tin trader Joseph of Arimathea. Near Looe's Celtic Lammana Chapel, Aesop Rock was originally called Yesu Rock, where Jesus sunbathed while his uncle did business in Looe; and the two are said to have walked up the coast to Glastonbury to establish Avalon, using Rock's Jesus Well en route. Springs appeared in Culbone Wood and Moor Wood to provide drinking water when Joseph struck the ground with his staff.

In AD312 Emperor Constantine made Christianity the empire's official religion; but the Celtic "pagani" had their own gods and goddesses, strongly connected to the natural world, and a number of Romano-Celtic shrines were built or refurbished, many of them in the hillforts, considered by the pagans to be hallowed ground.

KING ARTHUR AND THE ANGLO-SAXONS

After almost four centuries of Roman rule, suddenly the British were on their own, with Saxon pirates making raids along the southern coastline. They appealed to Emperor Honorius to help them, but he could not spare the troops; so Vortigern, who controlled much of South East England, made a deal with the Germanic tribes being squeezed out between Romans, Huns and Goths, offering them land in exchange for military support.

Led by brothers Horsa and Hengist, the first wave of Anglo-Saxons arrived in three warships in AD449 and proceeded to take over, backed up by large numbers of reinforcements arriving from the continent. Gildas reported that they set fire to "all the neighbouring cities and lands… until it burnt nearly the surface of the whole island, and licked the western ocean with its red and savage tongue." He went on to describe a great Romano-British leader whose twelve victories against the barbarians culminated in a final triumph on a battlefield known as Badon Hill, bringing fifty years of peace. The exact location of this battle is not known, but it is thought to be somewhere in the South West. Gildas doesn't name the British warleader, either; but later writers of medieval and Victorian romances had no doubt: this was the legendary King Arthur of Camelot.

Tintagel's claim to the King Arthur romance brings in huge flocks of visitors. The castle standing on Tintagel Island today was built in the thirteenth century by the Earl of Cornwall, but its history as a settlement is much earlier. The Iron Age promontory fort was refortified in the fifth century, when the Britons were under siege from the Anglo-Saxons, while the quantity and quality of Mediterranean pottery found here show that the castle was the stronghold of a powerful warlord with extensive mineral reserves – but was it King Arthur?

ST NECTAN'S KIEVE

King Arthur's round table is said to be buried beneath the Norman motte and bailey at Bossiney Mound, and when Arthur returns one midsummer night with his knights, the table will rise out of the mound for their use. The ceremony turning the men into knights took place at St Nectan's Kieve, above Rocky Valley. As the men passed through the rock arch they were reborn, and when they dropped to the pool below they were cleansed of sin. One of the many sixth-century missionary offspring of the Welsh King Brychan of Brycheiniog, Nectan had a hermitage at the top of the kieve. Today his wood is noted for its rare mosses and liverworts.

LANDS END

Off the tip of Land's End, the Seven Stones granite reef was traditionally known as "The City", and offshore old stone walls have been spotted underwater. In Arthur's day, when sea levels were some 20 metres lower than today's, it was part of Lethowsow, said to be a fertile land with many prosperous villages and 140 churches. Was it Lyonesse?

The reef's seven peaks are visible only at low tide, and they are particularly hazardous to shipping. No fewer than 71 shipwrecks have been recorded here, including the 1967 *Torrey Canyon* disaster, when a tanker with a full cargo of crude oil was heading to Milford Haven from Kuwait. The spillage was so extensive that eight Lossiemouth Buccaneers were scrambled to bomb the tanker to the seabed, and then RAF Hunter jets flew in from Chivenor to set the oil alight to clear the slick.

CHOUGH

According to medieval manuscripts, Arthur's last battle was at a place known as Camlann. After the battle, Arthur and his men fled west across Lethowsow, reaching the Scilly Isles just before the sea rose to cut them off. Arthur had been fatally injured, however, and Sir Bedivere was sent to cast Excalibur into the waters of Loe Pool. After Arthur had taken his final breath, his soul flew away in the body of a chough, whose red beak and legs are said to symbolise his fatal wounds.

Cornwall's national bird disappeared from England in 1973, after the Victorians hunted it for sport and later its habitat was spoilt by intensive farming methods. Like the ancient Britons, choughs had withdrawn to the Celtic fringes, and Cornwall was their last stronghold in England. In 2001, three choughs were sighted in the county and the following year a pair nested in a sea cave here. The Cornwall Chough Project was established, and a team of RSPB staff and volunteers kept a round-the-clock watch on the nest, resulting in today's healthy colony on the Lizard.

GIANT'S HEDGE

"Jack the giant, having nothing to do, built a hedge from Lerryn to Looe." One of the largest ancient earth banks in the UK, Giant's Hedge stretches some nine miles and in places is more than 4m high and 7m wide. It can be seen in Looe's Kilminorth Woods – a nature reserve that has been continuously wooded for more than 400 years – and is thought to have enclosed the territory of a Celtic chieftain driven west by the Anglo-Saxons. The giant Bolster built a similar bank below St Agnes Beacon, enclosing the headland between Chapel Porth and Trevaunance Cove. Its name comes from the Cornish "both lester", meaning "boat-shaped hump". This was probably also built by a tribal chief to defend his land from the Anglo-Saxons, who resumed their relentless progress through the land after the Badon Hill battle. When they reached the Bristol Channel, the Britons divided into two bodies – those who withdrew northwards into Wales and beyond, and those who went southwards, into the place known then as West Wales (today's Cornwall).

TRISTAN STONE

Sometime in the sixth century, the Tristan Stone was moved from a local Bronze Age henge to its current position beside the road into Fowey. On the reverse is inscribed a T (an early form of the Christian cross), while the front says (in Latin): "Here lies Tristan, son of Cunomorus". Cunomorus (King Mark of Cornwall), was born in 460 and had a base at nearby Castle Dore. The Iron Age hillfort was later refortified, and archaeologists found traces of a wooden hall inside its stone walls, believed to have been King Mark's feasting hall. Mark's grandson, King Gereint, lived above the western shoreline of Gerrans Bay, in Dingerein Castle. He was killed at the Battle of Catterick in 598 and buried in a golden boat with silver oars on Carne Beacon, above the Romano-British "Ringaround" settlement. Novelist Daphne du Maurier lived in Fowey, as did Arthur Quiller-Couch (known as "Q", whose monument can be seen on Fowey's Hall Walk). Q died before he could finish his telling of the Tristan and Isolde story (entitled *Castle Dor*), so du Maurier finished it for him.

THE CELTIC SAINTS

The Roman Church was beginning to establish monasteries throughout Europe, and in 590 Pope Gregory dispatched Saint Augustine to do the same in Britain. Meanwhile, St Patrick was sending out missionaries from Ireland to support Celtic Christianity in pagan Britain. In the Hayle RSPB bird reserve a 1999 stone erected by St Germoe Church celebrates 1500 years of Christianity following the landing of a party of Irish evangelists on Porthkidney Sands. In time the oratories founded by saints Ia, Anna, Euny and others evolved into chapels and then churches that are still in use today throughout the St Ives area.

CHAPEL PORTH
The sixth-century Celtic missionaries arrived on the shoreline in a fleet of unlikely vessels. Saint Ia was washed up near St Ives on a leaf (believed actually to have been a coracle), while St Carantoc steered an altar on to the beach at Crantock. Saint Piran chose a millstone to bring him across the Irish Sea, fetching up on Chapel Porth beach near Perranporth. Here he set up a hermitage for himself at Chapel Rock, where there was a spring nearby to provide drinking water and a makeshift font. Taking his mission out into the heathen community, he soon gathered a huge following, requiring his small hermitage to be upgraded to an oratory in the dunes.

Another party of Celtic saints, led by saints Piran and Carantoc, landed at Perranporth to establish a Christian community here. St Piran's sermons were hugely popular, and gradually his oratory was enlarged and improved. A small lake nearby originally prevented the chapel from being overwhelmed by sand, but in time this drained away and the oratory was buried. Eventually a new church was built further inland, later becoming Perranzabuloe Parish Church. St Piran died at the age of 200 when he fell into a well near Bossiney after a drinking session with St Nectan, and his head was carried around the county in a sacred reliquary. He was reputedly a huge man; and archaeologists excavating the complex multi-period cemetery in the dunes found a gigantic headless skeleton.

Other prehistoric remains unearthed here included Neolithic bones and Iron Age cists. Medieval plague victims were among the later burials, as well as canons from the collegiate church founded in the thirteenth century by Bishop Briwere of Exeter. Established around Carantoc's hermitage and known as Langorroc, this church became an important pilgrimage site, until the monastery's fabulous wealth from its mineral reserves led the monks into ungodly ways, and Langorroc was buried in sand in an act of divine retribution.

Over the centuries other churches on the north coast were swamped by windblown sand. In Gwithian, St Gothian's Chapel was buried three times, and between the sixteenth and nineteenth centuries St Enodoc chapel was so inundated that the vicar and his parishioners had to descend through the sacristy roof. In Padstow they blame the mermaid who fell in love with local lad Tom Yeo. Mistaking her for a seal (or so he said), he shot her, and in her fury she called up a great sandstorm that swept up the estuary creating the famous Doom Bar.

Other mermaids lurk in Cornwall's Atlantic waters. At Sennen the rocky islet known as the Irish Lady is named after the sole survivor of a wreck, who was seen clinging to the rock but drowned before help could reach her. Look out for a lady perched on the rocks with a rose in her mouth. A few miles away, Pendour Cove is also known as Mermaid's Cove, and if you sit above the cove at twilight on a summer's evening you may hear the sad song of the man who fell in love with the Mermaid of Zennor. This is also a very good place for seal spotting.

At Hartland, where St Nectan had a second hermitage, a swineherd gave him two cows as a reward for helping him find some lost pigs. When the cows were later stolen, Nectan located the thieves and tried to convert them; but remaining devoutly pagan, they beheaded him. Undeterred, he picked up his head and carried it back to his well before he collapsed and died, and his bloodstains were marked by foxgloves.

Another saint who carried his head back to his hermitage after a beheading was the Irish saint, Wyllow, who lived across the river from Fowey. Murdered by a kinsman, he too had

LUNDY HOLE

In Wales, a yellow fever epidemic prompted a mass exodus to Europe via Cornwall and Brittany. This included King Brychan's 24 missionary offspring, among them St Minver, who was visited by the Devil as she sat combing her hair near Port Isaac. She threw her comb at him with such force that he fled to the sea cave at "Topalundy, where on a round high hill there is a strange deep hole there made by the Devil in avoiding St Menfre". Saints Meva and Issey set up their hermitage at Mevagissey, while St Endellion's patch was near Port Isaac. Morwenna preached at Morwenstow, where she had to climb the sheer cliffs with the boulders needed to build her hermitage at the top. From here she still had sight of her Welsh homeland, across the Bristol Channel. In her last days, her brother Saint Nectan raised her up on her deathbed so that she could see the Brecon Beacons once more before she died.

a steep climb back to his hermitage, where he finally fell. His blood stained the hedgerows scarlet where he walked. Daphne du Maurier was married in the church later built in St Wyllow's parish, and it featured as "Lanoc Church" in her novel, *Rebecca*. Another literary connection was Kenneth Grahame, who wrote *Wind in the Willows* while staying in the area with his friend "Q".

Right:
SELUS STONE

Hermitages were established in Penwith by saints Just and Levan, great-grandsons of St Constantine. St Levan's well is preserved above a beach near Porthcurno and reached by means of a flight of ancient granite steps. In the medieval churchyard above, his followers erected a tall cross beside a pagan stone in order to sanctify it. St Levan struck the cross with his staff, causing it to split in two, and declared that if anyone succeeded in leading a loaded packhorse through the two halves, it would mean that the world was about to end. In St Just, the Selus Stone bears the ancient Christian chi-rho symbol, the sign of a very early ministry. The symbol can also be seen above the door of the church in Phillack, and on a stone outside St Anthony of Meneage. Meneage means "land of monks", and another of the great medieval monasteries was founded here.

Below, far right:
CRISTEL MAEL

The three-holed cross in the dunes at Perran Sands marked ancient territorial boundaries, and a tenth-century document referred to it as the "Cristel Mael". Although this is one of only two three-holed crosses in Cornwall, there are more than 400 ancient stone crosses of other designs in the county, and the fragmented remains of 200 more. One or two date from the late Neolithic or early Bronze Age and were later adapted by Christians. Most commonly, wayside crosses showed the safest river crossings or stood beside paths, highlighting a pilgrimage route or marking the way to "lans", the earliest holy sites. In later medieval days they were erected in the memory of local chieftains, or marked boundaries and market places. On the coast – for example Punche's Cross beside Polruan's eighth-century St Saviour's Chapel – crosses were sometimes used to warn sailors of hazardous rocks. In chapels and hermitages on cliffs and headlands, monks kept a light burning through the night for the same purpose.

ALFRED AND THE VIKINGS

By the beginning of the seventh century the Anglo-Saxons had established the main regions which later came to constitute England. This included Wessex, but not the highlands and remote areas, where the Britons still held out against the invaders, who also exploited the region's mineral wealth but otherwise left it alone.

In 669 an Archbishop of Canterbury was appointed to tour England and lay down the ground rules of the Roman church. Over the next few centuries, various kings gave a sizeable acreage to the Church in return for a promise of eternal salvation, and a number of powerful monasteries were established throughout the region.

Many of the monasteries were on the coast, and their great wealth made them a tempting target for sea raiders. At the end of the eighth century three Viking ships put in at Portland, killing the Reeve of Dorchester (who thought they came in peace) and heralding two centuries of Viking harassment. In 835 a Danish fleet landed on English shores, and the following year 25 Viking ships sailed up the Bristol Channel, defeating King Ecgbert and his men in a bloody battle at Carhampton. Three years later, when Ecgbert was expanding his territory, Vikings fought alongside Britons in Cornwall, where their defeat at Hingston Down resulted in the final loss of Cornish independence.

There were more battles, at Portland in 840 and Carhampton in 843. In an 845 battle on the River Parrett, "the men of Dorset took the victory", and in 851 a Devon army defeated the Danes; but in 865 a vast Viking army raged through the land in a campaign of rape and pillage. Wessex alone was able to hold out against them; but in 870 the Danes made a determined bid for the South West coast.

Following the Saxons' success at Countisbury, Alfred's army went on to defeat the Danes, who settled in East Anglia, where they converted to Christianity and became farmers. Coastal raids continued from new waves of Danish invaders, however, and it took the men of Appledore over a year to repel an 892 Viking landing party. Longboats landed at Port Quin, where one is still buried beneath the sand. A party of Danes was slaughtered at Bantham, but others mounted successful operations at Berry Head and at Pendennis; while at Abbotsbury the fifth-century church dedicated to St Peter, sacked by Saxon pirates, was destroyed again, this time by Viking raiders. Alfred built himself a strong navy to head off the Danes at sea; but raids continued on coastal settlements, including Porlock in 914.

ST ALDHELM'S CHAPEL
The medieval chapel at St Aldhelm's Head stands within a low circular earthwork, thought to be an early Christian site. Eighth-century Abbot of Malmesbury and Bishop of Sherborne, St Aldhelm was the first Anglo-Saxon to write in Latin. Nonetheless, he would stand on a bridge and sing in Old English, and when a crowd gathered to listen he started preaching, still in song.

STUDLAND CHURCH

At Studland, one of England's finest Norman churches was built to replace the Saxon church destroyed by Danes in the ninth century. Holed up behind their timber-faced ramparts in nearby Wareham – an important cross-Channel port in Saxon times – in 876 the Anglo-Saxons were compelled to make a deal with the 2000-strong army surrounding them. The Danes nonetheless killed their hostages and under cover of darkness sneaked away to Exeter. A fleet heading westwards to support them was caught in a storm at sea, and 120 ships were lost off Swanage. Alfred's men pursued the mounted force to Exeter but were unable to penetrate their fortress and again had to negotiate a deal. Early in 878 the massed Vikings set up their base in Chippenham and Alfred withdrew to the Somerset Levels.

WIND HILL

According to the Anglo-Saxon chronicles, in 878 "Hubba the Dane landed in Devonshire, with three and twenty ships, and there was he slain, and eight hundred men with him, and forty of his army. There also was taken the war-flag, which they called The Raven." This battle took place on Countisbury's Wind Hill, where the massive ramparts of the Iron Age hillfort made use of the deep East Lyn Gorge to the rear as well as the high seacliffs. The Vikings were heading up the Bristol Channel to flush out Alfred; but from the Saxon camp at the top of Wind Hill, Odda's men spotted them long before they landed at Porlock. The Danes marched overland to Countisbury, bedding down for the night by the narrow neck of land which was the Saxons' only way out. Assuming that Odda's men had limited provisions, Hubba planned to starve them out; but forewarned, the Saxons slaughtered the Danes as they lay sleeping.

ANGLO-SAXON ENGLAND

In 927 Athelstan put down a rebellion from the Welsh and Cornish, restoring the Roman walls around Exeter and setting up a royal household there. Cornwall's King Huwal attended Athelstan's celebration party, but in 931 he tried to reclaim his land from the king. Despite a coalition with some Danes he was again easily defeated, and Athelstan conquered the Scillies too. Declaring himself King of all England, he set the Welsh border on the River Wye and the Cornish border on the Tamar, and established a Bishopric at St Germans.

When Ethelred the Unready acceded to the throne, Viking fleets again ransacked England's shores, taking captives for the lucrative slave trade overseas and plundering the coastal settlements. There are records of raids on Starehole Bay and elsewhere along the South Devon coast. Padstow was sacked in 980 and Portland in 982; in 997 Devon and Cornwall suffered particularly badly, as did Dorset in 998. Devon was again hammered in 1001 and 1002, and by 1013 the Danes held most of southern England.

In the eleventh century, the spirit of St Nectan rescued Earl Godwin from a shipwreck at Hartland. Godwin's wife Gytha celebrated his survival by establishing a collegiate church of 12 canons on her lands at Hartland manor. In 1052, en route from Ireland, her son Harold landed with nine ships at Porlock, plundering the town and setting fire to it before proceeding to London to claim the English throne. In 1066 the same Harold Godwinson arrived at Hastings, "on his horse, with his hawk in his hand" in his doomed bid to protect his realm from the Norman Conquest.

ST BEUNO'S SAXON WINDOW
At Culbone, Exmoor, England's smallest church still in use was built on the site of a tenth-century Saxon church, itself established on St Beuno's sixth-century hermitage. Rebuilt in the twelfth century, the church features a small carved window salvaged from the original Saxon building. A lepers' squint was added later to allow the Culbone leper colony to partake in services without infecting the congregation. Throughout history, various outcasts were banished to Culbone Wood, including witches, criminals and the insane. Later Culbone communities included charcoal-burners, eighteenth-century slaves from the sugar plantations who won their freedom after 21 years, and a small group of romantics fleeing the Industrial Revolution, who were completely self-sufficient for two generations.

HOLYWELL CAVE

At Holywell, St Cuthbert's Well is in a beach cave, accessible only at the lowest of tides. Here, spring water dripping through the rock over thousands of years has created a spectacular "speleotherm" – a pillar built in a series of calcium carbonate basins. After the disastrous 793 Viking raid on Cuthbert's monastery at Lindisfarne, his remains had been moved to Durham for safety. Following the 937 uprising of Celts and Vikings, a later Bishop of Lindisfarne exhumed the saint's body again, intending to take it to Ireland; but a storm in the Irish Sea drove his boat on to Holywell beach. As the bishop took shelter in the cave, St Cuthbert's healing powers were transferred to the spring, and for many generations sickly children were brought here to be healed.

CORFE CASTLE

Corfe Castle was one of William I's early strongholds. There was a wooden fort in Alfred's time, built on a Roman defensive site, and its location meant that no-one could pass unnoticed between North and South Purbeck. In the thirteenth century King John added a great hall and a chapel, and his son, Henry III, strengthened it by adding walls, towers and gatehouses. Elizabeth I sold it to her dancing master, and in 1635 it was sold to the Lord Chief Justice, Sir John Bankes.

4
AFTER THE CONQUEST

THE DOMESDAY BOOK

AFTER HIS VICTORY at Hastings, William I marched to Exeter, where Harold's mother and his three illegitimate sons were living. He took the city after an 18-day siege and marched into Cornwall, handing it to his half-brother, Robert de Mortain, with much of Somerset too. Later William built castles in key locations, but few were in the South West. Portland's first Rufus Castle belonged to redhead William II, and rebel baron Stephen of Blois built the twelfth-century Rings earthwork to mount a siege on Corfe Castle, held by supporters of Henry I's daughter and heir, Matilda. Boscastle's Bottreaux Castle was built during the reign of Henry II.

When William I drew up the 1086 Domesday Book (helped by William Giffard of Devon), most of Cornwall belonged to the Church, including the Collegiate Canons of Perranzabuloe's St Piran and Bodmin's St Petroc (relocated from Padstow – "Petrocstowe" – to escape Viking raids). Penwith's Carn Brea was topped by a Neolithic monument and a medieval chapel.

Tehidy was owned by the Basset family; Lanherne and Caerhays belonged to the Arundells; Treago to the Treagos, who built Crantock Church's fourteenth-century aisle; and Trelawne to the Trelawneys. Stowe Barton later became the Grenville family's estate.

Devon's only Domesday coastal settlement was Barnstaple, established by Athelstan in 930 and minting coins twenty years later. The king gave Salcombe Regis to the monks of Exeter, who worked its saltpans and had a summer residence in Branscombe. Paignton and Bigbury both had a salthouse, and Seaton had 11. The Abbot of Otterton Priory employed 33 salters at Budleigh Salterton and his mill at Otterton – still grinding corn today – was mentioned in the Domesday Book as the most important of the valley's 70 water mills.

The Branscombes' Seaton home was built on a ledge above a valley and was fortified, as was Mortehoe's Damage Barton. Lee Abbey (not an abbey at all but a Victorian gentleman's residence) was built on the Domesday manor of Ley, owned by Thorncombe's Forde Abbey,

ST GERMOE'S CHAIR

Keen to keep God on their side, the Normans built large numbers of churches, many on the sites of earlier chapels. Near Praa Sands, St Germoe's Church was constructed from Tregonning granite, and the fourteenth-century monkeys flanking the entrance symbolised evil spirits being driven out. In the graveyard, St Germoe's Chair was rumoured to contain the saint's bones, but it was found to be empty. Landing at Hayle with a party of Irish missionaries in 460, Germoe and his sister Brecca had been chased away by a local warlord and set up their mission here instead.

and Henry III gave Countisbury and Lynton to Forde Abbey too. Countisbury had a much larger population than today, with extensive farming, and there was a settlement at Desolate, near Foreland Point. Chambercombe manor and Tapeley Park were also listed in the Domesday Book, as was Dannonchapel.

Exmoor was a royal hunting forest. Porlock's Holnicote – later the family seat of the Aclands – is listed, and the oldest part of Minehead, Quay Town. Dunster Castle belonged to William de Mohun, whose support at the Battle of Hastings was rewarded with 69 manors, including Fowey's Hall Manor. Dunster was sold to the Luttrell family in the fourteenth century, and the Burgundy Chapel on Minehead's North Hill was built in thanksgiving for a Luttrell's safe return from the Burgundian Wars a century later. Medieval settlements at East and West Myne, listed as belonging to William de Mohun, pre-dated Domesday, and there are still traces of their fields, including a water meadow, where winter rainwater was collected for growing early crops.

Over a third of Dorset belonged to the Church, which boasted nine monasteries. The only coastal settlement was Lyme Regis, whose fishermen paid 15 shillings to the monks of Sherborne Abbey for their fish and whose 13 saltworkers paid 13 shillings for the salt. There were also 32 salthouses in Studland. Tyneham belonged to Robert de Mortain and was known as "Tigeham", possibly meaning "goat enclosure".

Dorset's pre-Domesday hamlet of Stanton St Gabriel was inhabited until the eighteenth century, when it was abandoned after the menfolk found jobs in the rope-making industry in Bridport and a cliff fall caused the coach road to be diverted inland. The medieval chapel was destroyed during the Reformation, but in 1650 the village's 23 families asked for it to be reinstated as their parish church. Another Dorset settlement was abandoned at West Ringstead, possibly as a result of the fourteenth-century Black Death, which entered Britain there.

THE MEDIEVAL LANDSCAPE

A rare remnant of the medieval field system, Braunton's Great Field is still farmed today in narrow, unfenced strips of land, each one furlong long and one chain wide (about 200x20m). Every landowner had several strips, and if they were adjacent he could enclose them with a hedge; but the fair division of land between Braunton's four manors meant that he rarely could, preserving the system long after most strips had been merged into larger fields. Strip fields can still be seen on the north coast at Croyde, Bossiney and Forrabury. On

ABBOTSBURY SWANNERY
Possibly the only place in the world where you can walk through a colony of mute swans – and a Harry Potter film location – Abbotsbury's Swannery was established in the eleventh century by the monks of St Peter's Abbey, who bred the birds for their lavish banquets. Early in the eleventh century King Canute's steward, Orc, founded the Benedictine monastery around the fifth-century hermitage regularly "visited" by St Peter. He was later granted the seashore bordering the abbey grounds, as well as the rights to all its shipwrecks. The abbey's wealth increased still further a few centuries later, when Nichola de Montshore was granted estates "by service of counting the King's chessmen and putting them in a box when he had finished playing with them".

89

Portland, they are known as "lawnsheds". On the Lizard, Ruan Grade's strip fields have been designated an "Area of Anciently Enclosed Land".

Later, fields were enclosed using ditches, banks, hedges and fences, constructed of whatever materials were available locally. Around Kelsey Head there are cornditches, where a high stone wall facing outwards discouraged the animals from entering, but a gently sloping bank on the inside made it possible for them to escape if they did.

CURZEYWAY

Unlike Dorset's smooth brick-like limestone, which can be laid in regular courses to form walls, Cornwall's slates are thin and brittle, making the traditional "curzeyway" herringbone pattern the best way to stack them. In coastal areas "sheep creeps" are let into the walls, allowing sheep but not clumsier cattle out on to the clifftops. In West Penwith, the hard granite is most easily managed in large blocks. A number of different stiles have evolved as a result, including "cattle stiles", where several longitudinal slabs are built into a low step ladder, and "coffen stiles" (from the Cornish meaning "artificial hole"), where the slabs are laid out on the ground like an outsize cattle grid.

The Normans introduced warrens to breed rabbits for the table and for their fur, and these "pillow mounds" can be seen around the coastline. Hartland's ruined folly, "The Pleasure House", was originally a sixteenth-century warrener's house.

At Duckpool, near Bude, winter storms in the 1980s exposed two medieval hearths preserved in the silt, with limpet and whelk shells layered between ashes and charcoal.

Traces of medieval oyster beds have been found at Gillan, and at Lynmouth and Porlock. By the ninth century the people on the Bristol Channel shoreline were also using beach cobbles to build V-shaped fish weirs across the foreshore, placing baskets to trap fish on the falling tide, utilising the world's second highest tidal range. Both places later became famous for their oysters, which were dredged up in the bay and kept in the old fish weirs until they were needed. At Porthgwarra, St Just miners excavated a tunnel to give access to tidal "hulleys" built in the rocks to store shellfish in the same way. Porthgwarra's second tunnel enabled farmers to gather seaweed for fertiliser.

Ferries established at the major river crossings remain in use today. Greenway's ferry across the Dart is still summoned by ringing a bell, but downstream, today's chain-drawn vehicle ferry replaced the boat that previously transported horses and carts as well as passengers. Before the construction of Ferry Bridge, at the eastern end of Chesil Beach, the only alternative to walking the 18 miles of Chesil shingle was a ferry hauled by rope between the Fleet and Portland harbour.

The earliest bridges – stone slabs across the water, known as "clam" or "clapper" bridges – were superseded by packhorse bridges. Sidmouth's only bridge until 1817 was Sidford's Norman packhorse bridge, and Newlyn's bridge was built in the twelfth century, as was one of its quays.

Bideford's Long Bridge was built in 1286, with 24 pointed arches of assorted spans according to the length of timbers available to its builders. The oak woodland growing along the Torridge supported a thriving shipbuilding industry, and the estuary had a lively maritime trade. The 16 arches of Barnstaple's 1280 Long Bridge were equally diverse. Major repairs were carried out in 1333, and again in 1437. Barnstaple was an important staple port, exporting wool and pottery from its two quays.

Ilfracombe was the embarkation point for the Normans in their wars with Ireland, as Dartmouth was for Richard the Lionheart's fleet leaving for the third crusade. Mousehole's 1389 quay was the landing place for the Knights of St John on their return from the Holy Land. Another important medieval quay served the Gannel, at Penpol ("head of the creek"), later known as the Port of Truro. Goods landed here were taken by cart or packhorse up the track to Trevemper, an important commercial centre at the river's tidal limit, where the packhorse bridge stands today.

Although a ferry crossed the Avon at Aveton Gifford, on the ancient route between Modbury and Kingsbridge, at low tide travellers had to ford the river between North and South Efford (named from "ebb ford"). The medieval bridge standing today was probably

FROE TIDAL MILL

By medieval times, wind and water were being used to power machinery. The causeway at Roseland's Froe once served to dam the creek, harnessing tidal power. Sluice gates in the dam, letting in water on the rising tide, were closed once it had turned, releasing a steady stream to power the mill. At nearby Polingey the monks' tidal mill was still working in 1812, and at Place House the front lawn was reclaimed from a tidal mill pond. Looe's Millpool causeway was built around 1600 for a tidal mill.

PONT PILL MILL

The water mill at Pont Pill, near Fowey, stands by St Wyllow's Bridge, documented in the fifteenth century. Named from the Cornish for "bridge", Pont provided quay facilities for the area's scattered farms and settlements. On a rising tide, barges carried out fresh produce from the farms and brought in timber and stone.

built by the Chichesters in order to travel between their Aveton and Stadbury manors without having to wait for the tide. The Rector of Churchstow bequeathed 100 shillings to the project in 1427, and a few years later the Bishop granted indulgences to those contributing to the its building and maintenance. The arch nearest the village once held a statue of the Virgin Mary, and was known as "Lady Arch".

Bridport exported wool, but most of its wealth came from making ropes, using locally-grown flax and hemp, crafted in the town's "spinning walks" in the long back gardens. In 1385 merchant John Huddersfield obtained permission from Richard II to collect a ha'penny toll for every horse-load of goods imported or exported, and the proceeds went to the construction of a harbour, built around the end of that century.

The most extensive building projects were still the churches and monasteries. One of the earliest, St Anthony in Meneage's 1150 church is said to have been built by shipwrecked Normans grateful for their rescue. It is particularly noted for its tin carvings, painted to look like wood. Rame church – today lit only by candlelight, with one of the last hand-pumped organs – was built around the same time, on land given by Earl Ordulf to Tavistock Abbey in the tenth century. On the Lizard, the now-ruined thirteenth-century St Rumon's Church was dedicated to a tenth-century Tavistock bishop, as was St Ruan's Well. St Rumon's had a "plein an gwarry" – a medieval amphitheatre unique to Cornwall and used for mummers' plays and prayer meetings. Surviving examples can be seen in St Just and at St Piran's Round, near Perranporth. Open-air religious gatherings continued in Cornwall for many centuries, often in a field marked with a cross ("parc an grouse" in Cornish). Mullion's Angrouse Cliff was a forum for Wesleyan preachers from 1758–1762.

The medieval chapel on Looe Island (also known as St George's Island) was a popular place for pilgrims; but so many people drowned trying to reach it that a new Benedictine chapel was built across from it on the mainland, sometime around the twelfth century. The nearby Lammana Celtic chapel belonged to Glastonbury Abbey, although by the fourteenth century it was privately owned.

St Ia's Church in St Ives was built between 1410 and 1434 using Zennor granite, and the clear glass in its Fishermen's Aisle enabled fishermen to keep an eye on their boats in the harbour during the service. The chapel on St Ives Head was dedicated to St Nicholas, patron saint of fishermen, as was the chapel on Ilfracombe's Lantern Hill. Drake's Island, known in 1135 as St Michael's, had a small chapel on it, later dedicated to St Nicholas.

The wealth and power of monasteries continued throughout medieval times. Little Bindon was built in 1149 by Cistercian monks, who moved to Wool's Bindon Abbey in 1172. Hartland Abbey was granted to the Archdeacon of Poitiers for a monastery of regular Black Canons in 1169, and Normandy's White Canons built Torquay's Torre Abbey in 1196.

St Michael's Mount was granted to the French Benedictine abbey of Mont St Michel, and the chapel on its summit, built in 1135 by the French abbot Bernard le Bec, was dedicated to St Michael, patron saint of high places. In 1193 the island was seized on behalf of the Earl of Cornwall (later King John) by Henry le Pomeray, who disguised his men as pilgrims. In 1262 it became a major pilgrimage destination after four miracles allegedly took place there.

Boscastle's William of Bottreaux gave Minster Church to the monks of SS Sergius and Bacchus at Angers, and they established a small priory around it. The broadleaf woodland

MERMAID OF ZENNOR
In Zennor a bench end depicts the village's famous mermaid, who lured a local lad to a watery doom. Mortehoe's St Mary's Church has grotesque sea monsters carved on its bench ends. At Mullion's St Mellanus there is a thirteenth-century dogflap, and Manaccan's twelfth-century church is famous for the 200-year-old fig tree growing from the steeple wall. In Mawgan Porth's medieval church tower one of the eight bells dates from the thirteenth century, and one cracked bell remains of the original three medieval bells in Lansallos church, after the others were destroyed by drunken revellers in the nineteenth century.

surrounding the church is thought to be a remnant of the ancient wildwood, preserved by the monks' coppicing for timber. It shelters Cornwall's largest known colony of the Greater Horseshoe bat, providing a home for as many as 5% of the UK's entire population of this endangered species.

THE HUNDRED YEARS' WAR

When Edward III declared himself "King of England and France" in 1340, he found himself in conflict with his continental neighbours, with no navy to fight his cause. Major ports were required to provide ships and crew for crown service, and a 1326 shipping survey recorded a 40-ton vessel contributed by Noss Mayo. Dartmouth – in 1347 Devon's fourth richest port – supplied 760 men and 30 ships to the siege of Calais, making it the third largest contributing port in the country.

Edward also gave the merchants authority to "go to sea at their own expense to attack

POLRUAN BLOCKHOUSE
A pair of blockhouses built to enable a chain to be stretched across the Fowey proved to be inadequate when the French attacked in 1357, and a boom defence was added. Dartmouth had a "fortalice" to string a similar chain across the River Dart to Godmerock, and records show that Studland had a castle in 1381, since claimed by the sea.

and destroy the king's enemies". Importer of Bordeaux wines, fourteen times mayor and the inspiration for Chaucer's "Shipman", Dartmouth's John Hawley led frequent raids on French vessels and ports, drawing French reprisals.

Cremyll's West Stonehouse was burnt down in 1350, and in 1403 French pirate William du Chastel led another devastating raid on Plymouth. In response, John Hawley and Bristol seaman Thomas Norton together seized seven French merchant vessels in the Channel. The following spring, du Chastel returned with 2000 men and 300 ships; but it took him six days to assemble his unruly fleet at Blackpool Sands, giving Hawley time to co-opt women and peasants into his regular army and dig a water-filled ditch crossed by a narrow causeway. Greeted by showers of arrows from the archers and barrages of stones thrown by the women, the French were easily beaten back, and du Chastel was killed, with two of his brothers taken captive.

An important resource during the Hundred Years' War, Combe Martin had been declared a Royal Mine the previous century, and Edward III sent miners from the Pennines to work in the adits still to be seen around the area. In the fifteenth century, King Henry V commented that "the battles of Crecy, Poitiers and Agincourt were won in the shafts of Combe Martin". Although it was particularly noted for its silver, other minerals were mined here – manganese, iron, lead, zinc and copper – and later Henry VIII appointed a leading German mining engineer to oversee operations here and elsewhere in Devon, with a thousand men to help him.

THE TUDORS

In 1473 the Earl of Oxford held St Michael's Mount under siege for six months during the War of the Roses, and Kingsand was named after Henry VII's brief landing in 1483, during his attempt to overthrow Richard III. Fisher's Nose Blockhouse was built in 1490 to protect the Cattewater, and Dartmouth Castle – the first to be purpose-built for defence by cannon – was twinned with Kingswear Castle, across the river. Tehidy was sacked and rebuilt in 1493.

At Gorran Haven, Sir Henry Bodrugan of Bodrugan Barton built the 1475 St Just Chapel of Ease as a landmark for sailors. A notoriously brutal supporter of Richard III, Bodrugan was sent to kill Henry Tudor's henchman Sir Richard Edgcumbe of Cotehele. Edgcumbe escaped by hiding behind a tree and throwing his hat into the Tamar, so that Bodrugan's men assumed that he had drowned. When Henry Tudor finally became king, he despatched

PORTH NANVEN ADIT
Tin mines at Ballowall, Cape Cornwall, first recorded in 1584, were active at least a century earlier, using Bronze Age tin streaming methods. As ore ran out near the surface, shafts and tunnels were dug. At first the rocks were broken manually, and then techniques including fire-setting were employed until 1689, when gunpowder was introduced. By now there were many mining operations, including an antimony mine above Port Quin, and lead and silver mines near the Rumps. In 1580 the Cornish adviser to the Company of Mines Royal said of Tregardock, "I can show you ore in the rock there that beareth 5 oz of silver in the 100 of ore."

AN GOF SCULPTURE

In recognition of the special circumstances governing tin mining, in 1201 King John granted Cornwall a charter confirming their "just and ancient customs and liberties". The miners' Stannary Parliament was the only body with any jurisdiction over the Cornish people, who paid tax to the Crown until 1388, when it was paid instead to the Duke of Cornwall. Later, Edward I made the county exempt from tax over a certain threshold, in acknowledgement of its poverty. So in May 1497, when Henry VII imposed crippling taxes throughout England to fund his border skirmishes with the Scots, the Cornish were outraged at being taxed twice over for a cause they did not support. Led by St Keverne's blacksmith ("An Gof" in Cornish) and a Bodmin lawyer, an army of Cornishmen marched to London, gathering supporters on the way. By the time they reached Blackheath their army totalled 40,000 men; but they were unarmed and easily overpowered. Their leaders were executed and the others heavily fined. In 1997, the An Gof Sculpture Trust commissioned a sculpture from Coverack-based Terence Coventry to commemorate the uprising's 500th anniversary.

Edgcumbe to Gorran Haven to assassinate Bodrugan. With Edgcumbe in hot pursuit, Bodrugan fled to Turbot Point and jumped off the cliff into a boat waiting to take him to France. His estates were confiscated and handed over to Edgcumbe, whose family also acquired Mount Edgcumbe through marriage in 1493.

In the 1540s, at loggerheads with France, Henry VIII upgraded Edward III's castles guarding the Dart and the Fowey and set about building more artillery fortresses: at Pendennis Head and St Mawes; on Portland and at Sandsfoot, where he used stone from Bindon Abbey; on a rocky outcrop at Salcombe; and on Drake's Island, whose small fort protected Plymouth Sound's only deepwater route into Devonport dockyard. Sir Richard Grenville built Mount Edgcumbe's "Picklecombe New Bulwark" in 1545.

Another enemy was King John of Portugal, following Henry's divorce from Catherine of Aragon and his attempts to break up John's monopoly of the spice trade. When the Portuguese fleet's flagship was wrecked on the rocks at Gunwalloe, almost half the crew drowned, leaving the ship defenceless against looters. Pengersick's Lord of the Manor – whose Tudor castle still stands in Praa Sands – was one of the magistrates who refused to prosecute the offenders, prompting an international incident.

When Henry's men plundered and destroyed abbeys and churches in the Reformation, seizing their wealth, St Catherine's Chapel at Abbotsbury survived because it was an important beacon for seafarers, and Forde Abbey was voluntarily handed over to save it from demolition. Hartland Abbey was also surrendered to Henry, who passed it on to his Sergeant of the Wine Cellar at Hampton Court. Many of the smaller churches and chapels were converted to domestic or agricultural buildings, and Gorran Haven's chapel of ease became a fishermen's store.

Hostilities with the French and Spanish continued into Elizabeth's reign. In 1588 the approach of the Spanish Armada was first spotted from St Michael's Chapel on Rame Head, and a chain of warning beacons was lit to alert the English fleet, starting at St Michael's Mount. The many beacon sites included St Agnes, Dodman

WESTERN RISING
On the wall of the Roman Catholic Church in St Ives, a plaque commemorates the 1549 Western Rising, or Prayer Book Rebellion, which resulted in the death of many of the town's men and the hanging of its mayor. Religious discontent was rife after the Reformation, and a 1548 protest in West Penwith developed into widespread rebellion when the government imposed the English-language version of the Latin Book of Common Prayer on the population. Seeing it as a threat to their Celtic tongue, the Cornish people joined forces with the virtuous villagers of Sampford Courtenay; and in July 1549 almost 6000 men marched upon Exeter, holding the city under siege for six weeks until the Earl of Bedford arrived, slaughtering several thousand rebels.

Point, Salcombe's Marlborough, Kingston's Hoist Point, Selworthy and Thorncombe. The number of fires lit sent vital information: one meant that the enemy had been spotted, two signified that an invasion was imminent, and three announced: "Too late, they're here!"

More than 130 Spanish galleons sailed up the English Channel. Here they were routed by the English fleet, including five ships from Barnstaple and twelve from Dartmouth, with Devon's Francis Drake and John Hawkins among their commanders. The Armada fled northwards, rounding the Scottish coastline and heading back down the west coast to dash home across the Channel. They are said to have visited Kingsand and Cawsand, and there are claims (much disputed) that seven Spaniards shipwrecked on the North Devon coast settled and established a swarthy, dark-eyed dynasty at Bucks Mills. The many generations of the Braund family included the flamboyant "King" of Bucks Mills, a nineteenth-century fisherman who single-handedly saved the lives of no fewer than nine sailors, receiving several commendations for his bravery.

In 1595 the Spanish despatched four galleys and 400 men to reconnoitre the Cornish coast for a prospective retaliation. The soldiers posted in Penzance in anticipation of such a raid outnumbered the Spaniards; but seeing the ships they turned and fled, leaving Francis Godolphin, Deputy Lord Lieutenant of Cornwall, with just 12 men to defend the town. Under the Spanish bombardment three English ships were sunk and 400 houses destroyed. The Spanish went on to land at Spaniard's Point, setting fire to Mousehole and chasing the

HOPE COVE CANNON

As the Armada returned to the Channel following its defeat at the hands of the English fleet, storm winds drove a transport ship, fitted out as a hospital ship, on to Hope Cove's Shippen Rock. Initially sentenced to death, the 140 survivors were ransomed instead. The cannon above the cove dates from this time, as do the four on Clovelly's quay. Other galleons captured included the *Madre de Dios*, brought into Dartmouth with all her spoils, and the *Nuestra Senora del Rosario*, which was sailed in to Tor Bay.

villagers up to Paul, which was also burnt down. In a final gesture of defiance they seized some of Henry VIII's coastal cannon and mounted them on their own ships.

In Elizabeth's reign seafarers grew ever bolder, hungry for the rich pickings to be found in uncharted lands, bringing back exotic plant species, including the sixteenth-century Judas Tree outside Maidencombe Court, transplanted from Lebanon.

Famous for finishing his game of bowls on Plymouth Hoe before setting out to conquer the Armada, Sir Francis Drake lived in Buckland Abbey, where it is said his drum will sound should England ever face such a threat again. Drake's parliamentary seat was Bossiney, and he gave his 1584 election speech from Bossiney Mound. Brixham hosts a replica of the Golden Hind, used in his 1577–1580 circumnavigation of the globe.

On Plymouth's Hooe Lake, the Radford estate belonged to the Harris family, bankers and backers of both Drake and Raleigh, who left their booty here for safekeeping before handing it over to the queen. In 1588 Christopher Harris held a banquet to celebrate their Armada victory; it was here that Raleigh was imprisoned in 1618 before his execution.

Near Gerrans Bay, Rosteague Manor belonged to Reginald de Mohun, one of Raleigh's naval captains, and Dartmouth's Greenway – later owned by Agatha Christie – belonged to Humphrey Gilbert's family. Raleigh's stepbrother, Gilbert conquered Newfoundland on his way to attempt the North West Passage, leading to strong links between Dartmouth and the Canadian province. Limestone from Galmpton quarries, used for ballast, has been found in some of the earliest buildings in the New World, as well as in quays in France and Spain. A fleet of up to 150 vessels from the Dart sailed to the Newfoundland fishing grounds each season, salting and drying the cod before taking it to Europe's Catholic countries, where it was exchanged for wine, oranges and dried fruit. The Bridport fleet also fished Newfoundland waters, preserving the catch in the town salt house.

Another seafarer operating from the Dart was John Davis, who discovered the Falkland Islands. Four centuries later, Kingswear's Colonel H. Jones was posthumously awarded the VC for his role in preserving the islands as a British territory.

Sir Richard Grenville's house at Stowe Barton, later rebuilt, was described as a "huge rambling building, half castle, half dwelling house with quaint terraces, statues, knots of flowers, clipped yews and hollies". Admiral of the 1585 fleet responsible for establishing a military colony off the coast of North Carolina, Grenville left from Stowe on his last voyage in 1591.

Lord of the Manor of Bideford, Grenville created the Port of Bideford in 1575, building on the town's charter granted to an ancestor in 1292 and transforming it from a quiet

WALTER RALEIGH

Sir Walter Raleigh was born in Colaton Raleigh's Hayes Barton. Elizabeth's particular favourite, he was knighted in 1585 for putting down rebellions in Ireland and colonising Virginia. When he secretly married her lady-in-waiting, however, the two were imprisoned in the Tower of London, relocating to his estate in Sherbourne on their release. In 1594 he sailed for South America seeking the fabled El Dorado, a voyage which returned him to royal favour; but on Elizabeth's death in 1603 James I imprisoned him on a charge of treason and confiscated his lands. He was later released to conduct another expedition to find El Dorado; but after some of his men ransacked a Spanish outpost, James had him beheaded to preserve the fragile peace with Spain.

fishing town to a major trading centre. A 250-ton ship made in 1566 for an Exeter merchant was the first recorded vessel built on the Torridge, and John Leland noted that Bideford had an entire street of "smiths and occupiers for ship crafts". The town became the largest importer of tobacco, after Raleigh landed his first consignment here, and Fremington clay was used by pipe manufacturers in Bristol and London.

Clovelly's medieval harbour was extended to accommodate its frequent use by the three adventurers, who would often meet in the thirteenth-century Hoops Inn. In 1584 Grenville built Boscastle's harbour, making it a significant port; and Raleigh, Drake and Hawkins helped finance the harbour at Hartland Quay, which also did a lively trade with South Wales and other Bristol Channel ports. The force of the Atlantic gales meant that major work was continually required to keep it in good repair; as it was at Bucks Mills, where the 1598 quay was finally washed away, so that sailors had to land their boats on the beach. According to local tradition, the Devil tried to build a causeway to Lundy from Bucks Mills, but he gave up when his shovel broke, leaving the spit of rocks known as the Gore.

FISHING

In St Ives Bay – once the South West's largest fishing port – the fishing grounds were divided up into separate timeshare holdings known as "seines", a practice first recorded in thirteenth-century Gorran Haven. Two of a seine's three boats towed a large drift net between them, bringing the catch ashore under the guidance of the third boat's crew. In Polperro 40 large gaff-rigged boats known as "Polperro gaffers" towed the seine nets.

On the beach the villagers would scoop out the pilchards in "tucking nets", taking them to the fish cellars, or "palaces" (from the Cornish "palas" meaning an enclosed space). Here fish were packed into barrels between layers of salt and compressed using wooden beams weighted with boulders. The oil collected was used for cooking and in lamps.

The cottages on Roseland's Place Creek are converted pilchard cellars, where fish was processed before being exported across the Channel. Fowey's massive pilchard cellars in Readymoney Cove handled fish caught in St Austell Bay, and in one year alone 60,000 hogsheads of pilchards (more than 14m litres) were shipped. Sixteenth-century Plymouth merchants, keen to capitalise on the booming fish business in Kingsand, built cellars there from the local red volcanic rock. A 1567 Paignton survey listed 17 "cellars and fish houses in Rowneham", and on Wonwell beach an ivy-clad chimney still stands where fishermen used to boil their crabs and lobsters.

COVERACK FISHING VILLAGE
Like every cove on the Lizard where a handful of boats could be drawn up, Coverack was a fishing village. Penberth had a fleet of 15 boats which were hauled ashore by means of the capstan today preserved beside the electric winch, and Cadgwith claims the record for the most pilchards caught in two days – a staggering 1.3 million. Today fishermen still work from Cadgwith, catching crabs, lobsters, monkfish and conger eels.

CLOVELLY CHAPEL

At Clovelly, a good day's catch could be as many as 9,000 herrings, and on one record-breaking day the haul amounted to 400 donkey loads. In the eighteenth century there were a hundred herring boats in Clovelly, and an annual festival is still held to celebrate the "silver darlings". A traditional fisherman's cottage is preserved here, near the cottage where Charles Kingsley used to write. A neighbouring cottage belonged to "Crazy Kate" Lyall, who one stormy day in 1736 watched helplessly from her window as her fisherman husband was drowned in the bay. Overcome with grief she put on her wedding dress and walked out into the sea.

PORT GAVERNE PILCHARD PALACE

The cob-walled fish cellars still standing at Port Gaverne once handled 1.5 million fish a week. There are similar buildings at Port Quin, a hamlet sometimes known as "the village that died twice", where ivy has claimed the crumbling ruins of abandoned cottages. Sometime in the nineteenth century all the men drowned in a storm, and their wives and children returned to their families. In time the fleet regrouped, but the fish disappeared and the village was deserted again.

At the end of the summer, "huers" were posted on clifftops to look out for the arrival of the fish. When he spotted the shoals beneath the flocks of gulls that followed them, the huer would shout "hevva!" ("shoal!"). The Cornish scones known as "heavy cakes", originally baked to celebrate the fleet's good fortune, take their name from this, with raisins representing the fish and criss-cross scorings the nets. The St Ives huer's lookout sits beside the Coast Path near Carbis Bay; in Newquay and on Burgh Island medieval chapels were used. The huer's perch on Lizard Point was a group of rocks known as "The Chair", and Cadgwith's clifftop hut later became a coastguard lookout and signal station.

Repeated extensions of Mousehole's 1389 quay finally provided moorings for up to 66 mackerel drifters and between 40 and 50 pilchard boats. The villagers were close to starving one winter when a series of gales kept the boats in, and two days before Christmas Tom Bawcock decided to go out regardless. His heroic haul of seven different types of fish is commemorated in the local "Starry Gazey Pie", baked with the heads of assorted fish poking through the crust.

In the biggest potential catch in Lulworth's history, in 1785 a whale blundered into the cove, but it managed to evade capture. The last big mackerel shoal spotted here was in 1946, and today's two commercial boats bring in just crabs and lobsters. Chesil Beach fishermen – who at night were able to tell where they had landed from the size of the pebbles – no longer go out, but the shoreline is still popular with anglers.

Above Harlyn Bay, carved into the lintel of the old fish cellars are the words "Lucri Dulcis Odor" – "Profit Smells Sweet". During a particularly lean period in the sixteenth century, the family living in today's "Mother Ivey's Cottage" landed more fish than they could handle. Mother Ivey appealed to them to donate it to the starving people of Padstow; but instead they ploughed it into the field to fertilise their crops. Furious, she put a curse on anyone digging there; and the family's son died in a riding accident soon afterwards. In the 1970s a man using a metal detector in the field suffered a fatal coronary, as did the foreman of a water company later laying pipes there. The field has remained untouched since.

Britain's earliest trade links with Japan were established in Plymouth, and her packet ships ran from Falmouth, carrying passengers, bullion and government intelligence as well as the mail. Dartmouth's Royal Avenue Gardens were reclaimed to provide additional mooring space, and at Trevaunance Cove the lords of the manor ran up huge debts to finance a harbour which was washed away five times. On the Bristol Channel, Ireland's Earl of Tyrone was shipwrecked near Combe Martin, where an annual "Hunting of the Earl of Rone" festival still honours the event. In 1620 the Pilgrim Fathers set off in the Mayflower

POLPERRO FISH MARKET
Although most fishing villages still have one or two boats bringing in crab and lobster for local restaurants, few of the large fleets remain. Business is still lively in Polperro harbour, and Looe's daily catch has a live feed on the fleet's website. Newlyn's fishing fleet is one of the largest in the UK and its harbour boasts Britain's last commercial pilchard press.

to colonise the New World, looking in at Dartmouth and Newlyn. There were also more coastal raids, this time from Barbary pirates seeking slaves as well as booty, and the vulnerable settlements on the South Devon coastline moved inland again.

Some of the early ports and harbours, too, were beginning to move inland, as estuaries were choked with wind-blown sand, shingle washed in by the sea and silt brought down rivers from mining and other operations upstream. St Ives took over from Lelant as the main port on the Hayle, while Shaldon supplanted Ringmore on the Teign. Otterton's Anchoring Hill, today two miles inland, provided moorings for ships of up to 100 tons until a massive storm in the sixteenth century blocked the mouth of the Otter estuary with a large ridge of shingle and pebbles. Another one in 1824 swept the boats out to sea and turned the beach permanently from sand to shingle.

By the sixteenth century, the River Brit was so silted up that it was little more than a creek, and a basic pier was built on stilts at the mouth of the river in the 1670s. In 1721 the river was diverted, and Bridport Harbour became one of the busiest on the coastline, exporting wool and rope. Storm and shingle soon choked the harbour again, and following storm damage in 1824 parallel piers were built, with sluice gates to hold in enough water to wash away new shingle when the gates were opened.

From medieval times stream tin was recovered in the catchment area for Helston's River Cober, and for more than 100 years 30 mines operated here. Mine waste washed downstream formed Loe Marsh and prevented water from passing through the shingle barrier, causing flooding in Helston, and from time to time the bar was breached to allow the water to flow away.

In Looe, the pier constructed to prevent the river from silting proved ineffective, and in the nineteenth century local engineer Joseph Thomas designed the banjo pier instead, which was copied throughout the world.

THE ENGLISH CIVIL WAR

During the Civil War Barnstaple changed hands four times, and Bideford's Roundheads built Chudleigh Fort above East-the-Water. A stout Royalist, Hartland's collector of the king's "ship money" fortified his farm at Blegberry, leaving small holes in his thick walls for the firing of muskets. Royalists strengthened their defences throughout the region, including Portland Castle, one of only three Dorset Royalist strongholds. On the Dart, they built Gallants Bower and Mount Ridley; and at Salcombe Sir Edmund Fortescue spent £135 6s

11d on refortifying Henry VIII's castle, paying his labourers 10 shillings a day. It housed a garrison of 65 officers and two washerwomen, and he renamed it "Fort Charles".

Ringmore's Royalist rector built a small fort to defend Aveton Gifford's bridge; but when the Roundheads landed at Ayrmer Cove he was forced to hide in the church tower for more than three months before escaping to France. Noss Mayo made thirteen fishing boats available to the king's men for a siege on Plymouth, where the Earl of Essex and 8000 men had driven Royalist Bevill Grenville back into Cornwall but found themselves trapped between him and Charles, who had marched down to block him from the north.

In 1643 Grenville's troops camped near Bude, routing the Roundheads at Stamford despite being outnumbered two to one. The Cornish army marched north, taking Taunton, Bridgwater and Bath before helping win Bristol from the Roundheads, but casualties included Grenville himself. Heading home, nonetheless they took Dorchester, Weymouth, Portland, Bideford, Barnstaple, Exeter, and Dartmouth. Like many other Cornish churches, Lelant still proudly displays the king's 1643 letter thanking the parishioners for their support.

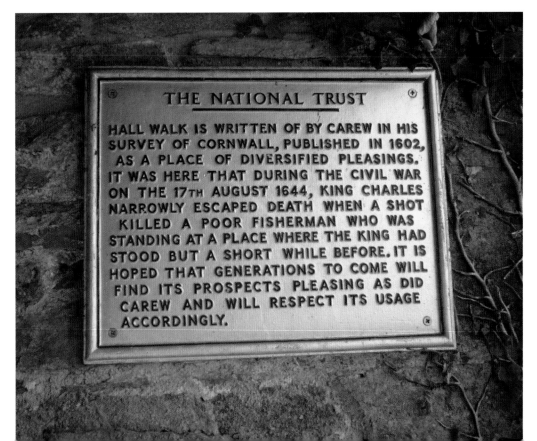

HALL WALK

The Fowey peninsula was occupied by Roundheads, led by the Earl of Essex, who holed up in the ruins of Castle Dore after the 1644 Battle of Lostwithiel. The Royalists took the hillfort in September, and Essex escaped to Plymouth in a fishing boat. Charles is said to have hidden out in an Iron Age fogou after his narrow escape on Fowey's Hall Walk.

CHIDEOCK MARTYRS' CROSS
Erected in 1645 in memory of five local men who died for their faith, Chideock Martyrs' Cross marks the site of the fourteenth-century castle destroyed by the Parliamentary forces 300 years later. After a mammoth battle, Abbotsbury Castle also fell to the Roundheads, who tossed burning faggots through the windows to drive out the garrison and then stormed the building, despite warnings that barrels of gunpowder were stored inside. When it blew up, 60 of Cromwell's men went with it. Corfe Castle survived a six-week siege and some half-hearted blockades, but in 1646 the Roundheads mounted their guns in the Rings earthwork and systematically destroyed the castle.

Near Veryan, Tregagle's Hole is said to be haunted by the ghost of an evil Wadebridge lawyer who spied for the Roundheads, summoned from the afterlife by a seventeenth-century court defendant seeking his testimony. Refusing to leave after the trial, Tregagle was set a series of tasks. Succeeding in emptying Dozmary Pool with a limpet shell, he fled to Roche Rock. In St Minver he had to weave ropes out of sand; but residents complained about his howling and he was moved on to Helston to carry sacks of sand from Bareppa to Porthleven. Here he was tripped by the devil and spilt sand across the mouth of the Cober, forming Loe beach; and so he was banished to Tregagle's Hole, where his wails can still be heard today.

Gallant's Bower hung on for some time before Fairfax took it for Cromwell, and the Royalist stronghold on St Michael's Mount left the Basset family when, on its surrender, Colonel John St Aubyn was appointed Governor of the island and later bought it. By 1646 Cromwell's men had the advantage in the South West, and Charles sought refuge in Pendennis Castle before sailing on to the Scilly Isles. The castle survived a five-month siege before surrendering to the Roundheads, as did Fort Charles, the last in England to hold out against Cromwell's men.

At West Bay the South West Coast Path shares part of its route with the Monarch's Way, a 615-mile long-distance footpath tracing the route of King Charles II's flight to France after his defeat in 1651, ending at Shoreham-by-Sea, where he took a boat to Europe.

In 1648, crippling taxes to fund military installations after the Civil War again led the Cornish to riot. Parliamentarians killed 70 Royalist rebels in Penzance, and 300 foot soldiers and 40 horsemen joined the 120 Mullion men marching over Goonhilly Downs to Mawgan-in-Meneage, before they were all defeated in a fierce battle at Gear Camp.

During the 1652 Anglo-Dutch Wars, a defensive tower was built on Mount Batten, and Plymouth's Royal Citadel was added soon afterwards. When Charles II died, the Duke of Monmouth (his illegitimate son) sailed into Lyme Regis to claim the throne from James II; but his Western Rebellion was put down at Sedgemoor and Monmouth and many of his followers were executed. George Jeffreys, the infamous "Hanging Judge", based himself in Penzance for the trial. High-ranking government rebels invited James's Dutch son-in-law to take up the English throne instead, and in 1688 William of Orange landed in Brixham with 20,000 men.

HAWKER'S HUT

The staunch loyalty of Pelynt Protestant Royalist Jonathan Trelawny was rewarded in 1685 when he was made Bishop of Bristol; but in 1688 he and six fellow bishops were imprisoned in the Tower of London for refusing to support James II's "Declaration of Indulgence", which granted Catholics religious tolerance. The "not guilty" verdict at their trial prompted national celebrations. When William of Orange landed in Brixham, James offered Trelawny the Bishopric of Exeter in return for his support. Declining, the bishop gave his allegiance to William, who took the throne and gave Trelawny the diocese himself.

Two centuries later the story of Trelawny and the Western Rebellion prompted the rector of Morwenstow to pen the Cornish national anthem, "Song of the Western Men." Hawker also introduced the harvest festival. A noted eccentric who invited his cats to church services but excommunicated them for mousing on a Sunday, the Reverend Hawker built himself a driftwood hut on the cliffs, where he would gaze out to sea, opium pipe in hand, on occasion accompanied by his friends Charles Kingsley and Alfred Lord Tennyson.

5

THE INDUSTRIAL AGE

IN 1791-2 DURGAN'S George Vancouver sailed two ships to Cape Town, Australia, New Zealand, Tahiti and China, surveying coastlines and collecting botanical samples. Proceeding to North America, his charts of its north west coast were so precise that they were used for coastal navigation for many generations.

Great discoveries were being made by academics too. In the leat of Manaccan's Tregonwell mill in 1791 the Reverend William Gregor discovered titanium, known then as Manaccanite. Ludgvan's Humphry Davy – a pioneer of electrolysis – invented the Davy Lamp, enabling miners to work safely in the presence of flammable gases, and Pendeen's William Borlase published tomes on Cornwall's natural history and archaeology. His great-great-grandson WC Borlase was also an archaeologist of note. Near Perranuthnoe, Stackhouse Cove – whose warm waters contain the widest range of seaweed species ever recorded in Britain – is named after marine biologist John Stackhouse, who catalogued them. He built Acton Castle above the cove for his sickly wife Susannah, and had a bath cut into the rocks, hoping that the sea air and the medicinal properties of seaweed would improve her health.

In 1712 Dartmouth ironmonger and engineer Thomas Newcomen devised a steam-powered Atmospheric Engine to pump out a mine shaft, and Scottish engineer James Watt's engine doubling the output on less than a third of the fuel was used in mines towards the end of the century. In 1771 Richard Trevithick, engineer at Ding Dong Mine near Land's End, designed a high-pressure steam engine that later became the standard source of power in the Cornish mines.

Near Mullion, Wheal Unity produced a record-breaking slab of native copper, 30 feet long and weighing 3 tons, and Perranuthnoe's Gundry family became so wealthy from their 1787 copper and silver mine at Wheal Neptune that they issued their own bank notes.

In 1798, a harbour was finally constructed at Trevaunance that could withstand the pounding waves, after four failed attempts had caused equal damage to the coffers. Ore was dropped by chute from the bins still visible on the clifftop, and coal was hoisted to the mines

Opposite:

BALLOWALL MINE SHAFT
Ballowall's cliffs are topped by a mine shafts, and many underground setts were working around Geevor by the eighteenth century. Named from the Cornish "Stennack an Gever" ("Tin Stream of the Goat"), its ingots were stamped with a fish-tailed goat. In Penzance, a mineshaft sunk below the high tide mark to exploit underwater tin reserves was drained using a 1791 steam engine onshore. The mine sold £70,000 worth of ore before an American ship broke its moorings and drifted on to the shaft head.

above by means of a winch drum powered by horses.

Horse whims were used in the slate mines, too, hauling dressed slates to the clifftops from the platforms below, although sometimes an aerial cableway known as a "blondin" was used instead. The remains of a working platform can still be seen at Dannonchapel. In the world-famous Delabole quarry, 1000 men produced around 120 tonnes of slate every day, which went to Port Gaverne on "The Great Slate Road". Each shipload was brought on 30 wagons pulled by more than 100 horses.

Portland was extensively sculpted by the quarryworkers, with deeply-grooved tracks linking settlements with countless quarries. Renowned for its hardness and durability, Portland Stone was used for UN buildings in New York and government buildings in New Delhi. In Britain, it was the stone of choice for the Palace of Westminster, St Paul's Cathedral, the Cenotaph and the Victoria and Albert Museum. It was also used for rebuilding London after the Great Fire of 1666.

TOUT QUARRY SCULPTURE
Portland's Tout Quarry was worked by members of the families who owned the "lawnshed" strips of land to the south. After 30,000 tons of boulders were quarried to build West Bay's sea defences, business ceased in Tout; and in 1983 the Portland Sculpture and Quarry Trust project took over. Many national and international artists have created sculptures within the quarry, which is now a protected landscape.

QUARRY WHIM
In Durlston's Tilly Whim quarries, workers extracted Purbeck Stone and split it into blocks using wedges and hammers, producing finished items such as troughs and sinks on site. A wooden whim lowered the finished stonework to the boats below, to be shipped directly to the Swanage Quay stoneyards or transferred to ketches anchored offshore. Purbeck stone was used for the fortification for the whole of England's Channel coastline during the Napoleonic wars; but demand for stone slumped afterwards, and the quarries closed in 1812. In 1887 George Burt opened Tilly Whim caves as a tourist attraction, but they were later closed for safety reasons. Today they provide an undisturbed roost for bats.

At Branscombe, Manor Mill was built in the eighteenth century on the site of an old grist mill. Rocky Valley's fifteenth-century Trevillet Mill was upgraded, and Boscastle's Valency valley is named from the Cornish "velenjy" (millhouse), built at the same time. In Appledore, the remains of a five-storey windmill built at the turn of the nineteenth century still stand on Windmill Hill. The Westcountry's first "flax swingling mill" was built in Burton Bradstock in 1803; and in Bridport, sails, sacking and tarpaulins were made using braiding machines.

Near Newquay, Cornish engineer John Edyvean built the first section of the St Columb Canal around 1774, funding it himself. He planned a 30-mile canal from Mawgan Porth to Newquay, using tub boats to bring in sand and seaweed; but the water drained away through the sandy soil and he abandoned the project. He also designed the Bude Canal, using pioneering engineering to connect Bude Harbour to the River Tamar via a 95-mile waterway, but Parliament took 40 years to approve it. Meanwhile, Lord Rolle was building an embankment beside the River Otter to channel its water along the eastern side of the estuary, which had silted up. Influential in the 1827 construction of the Torrington-Rolle Canal, Rolle planned another by the Otter; but major storm damage along the Budleigh seafront diverted his resources and it was never built.

ROMANTICS AND REVOLUTIONARIES

In St Agnes, a terrace of fine houses was built for sea captains at "Stippy Stappy" terrace, and in 1796–1887 shipyards built 200 vessels in the small fishing village of Salcombe, where Tennyson wrote the poem "Crossing the Bar" in a summerhouse. Here, as in Dartmouth, land was reclaimed to extend the foreshore, and on promenades throughout the South West tropical plants thrived in the warm air.

Landowners built sumptuous country houses with deer parks, follies and exotic gardens, introducing pretty but invasive species that later required culling – rhododendron, Himalayan balsam, Japanese knotweed. Lulworth Castle was developed from a seventeenth-

VALLEY OF ROCKS GOAT

Feral goats are a common sight around Lynton's Valley of Rocks – a favourite haunt of Romantic poets Coleridge and Wordsworth, who both lived in the Quantocks at the end of the eighteenth century. Coleridge was staying in Culbone's Ash Farm when his composition of "Kubla Khan" was famously interrupted by "a person from Porlock". Robert Southey was a frequent visitor, declaring that if landscape alone decided where he lived, it would surely be at Porlock, whose Ship Inn today boasts a "Southey's Corner". Another visiting friend was revolutionary John Thelwall, whose notoriety led to the three poets being accused of spying for the French during their nocturnal rambles on North Hill, after French support for Irish Republicans led to an invasion party landing on the Welsh coast.

century hunting lodge, and Buckingham Palace architect John Nash designed Caerhays Castle, with towers and follies in its formal gardens. The Hamlyns' family seat at Clovelly Court, built in 1740, was famous for its kitchen gardens, with peaches, figs and lemons growing among the vegetables and vines. The Basset family demolished the old house at Tehidy, replacing it with a Georgian gentleman's residence with extensive landscaped grounds. Cornwall's fourth largest landowners, they owned two of its most profitable mines and their annual mining revenue was £10,000.

Formal gardens were established at Mount Edgcumbe, and their many classical seats and follies, inscribed with poetry, enjoy spectacular views across the Tamar. Like Maker church, two were built from stone salvaged from West Stonehouse's medieval church. On the Erme, Modbury lawyer Christopher Savery built banks enclosing the marsh at South Efford so that he could graze livestock there, trebling the value of his property, and land reclaimed from the sea for grazing did the same at Braunton Marshes.

Portland's Governor John Penn built Pennsylvania Castle on the island in 1797, after his grandfather founded Pennsylvania and the city of Philadelphia. John fenced in land around Rufus Castle and St Andrew's church, prompting a public outcry that resulted in a court order requiring him to pay five shillings rent per annum for it. He also built a large stone bath above the cove, which his servants had to fill with buckets of seawater, but renewed public outrage forced him to abandon it.

In 1755 – commemorated in a headland near Land's End – Dr Samuel Johnson wrote the first Cornish Declaration of Independence, asserting Cornwall's rights to self-government as granted by the Stannary Charters, and William Wordsworth returned from the French Revolution with a strong social conscience. His friend Coleridge – a fervent preacher who walked from the Quantocks into Bridgwater and Bristol to give his sermons – teamed up with Poet Laureate Robert Southey to lay plans for a "Pantisocratic State" in America, based on the principles of equality, tolerance and self-government that underpinned William Penn's "Charter of Privileges".

THE NAPOLEONIC WARS

In 1795, amid fears of an invasion by Napoleon's army following the French Revolutionary Wars, lookouts and signal stations were established around the coastline to keep a watch for French ships, and work began on Torbay's coastal defences to protect the naval fleet anchored in the bay. Guns were based in Brixham, where the South Fort faced inland to

BOVISAND

In 1779, an enormous joint French and Spanish fleet anchored in Cawsand Bay, intending to take Rame Head to mount a campaign against Plymouth's Citadel and its dockyards. The city's defences were hopelessly outclassed by the 30,000 infantry with field guns in the invaders' 66 vessels, and it only escaped capture because easterly gales drove the fleet to the Scilly Isles, where the English Navy was waiting for it. Both forces retreated after a stand-off, but Tehidy's Francis Basset was so concerned that it might happen again that he marched his miners to Plymouth and set them to work, strengthening its fortifications. Bovisand's harbour and breakwater were built to enable ships at anchor to send longboats to collect water, and an underground pipe still leads from a large reservoir to the jetty.

QUEEN ADELAIDE'S GROTTO

Queen Adelaide's Grotto at Mount Edgcumbe was built around a cave used as a lookout. Edgcumbe's strategic position made it an important site for Plymouth's Napoleonic defences, and the 1758 Earl's Battery was joined in 1760 by the Redding Point Battery, constructed to cover the bridge channel and the west of Plymouth Sound. Following the 1775 War of American Independence, redoubts and barracks were established on Maker Heights. The Minadew Battery was completed in 1779 and was designed to cover the beaches, with the help of batteries at Cawsand and Sandway.

repel land-based attack, and Hardy's Head Battery – originally built in 1780 for the American War of Independence – covered Berry Head Fort. Today's Berry Head Hotel was converted from the military hospital (later the home of Brixham's popular vicar, Reverend Henry Francis Lyte, who composed the hymn "Abide With Me").

As the rise of Bonaparte triggered the Napoleonic Wars in 1803, the Royal Navy's "press gangs" forcibly co-opted fishermen from pubs and beaches around the South West coast. In their absence, when French ships were sighted heading up the Bristol Channel, Ilfracombe's womenfolk donned red petticoats and paraded on Capstone Hill, simulating troops on patrol.

In February 1804, HMS *Venerable* was on her way from Torbay to help blockade Brest when she was stranded and bilged on Paignton Ledges. The following year Lord Nelson's body was brought in to Falmouth after the Battle of Trafalgar. According to Thomas Hardy's "Trumpet Major", the white horse on the hillside above Osmington was carved to commemorate the battle. When France was finally defeated, a thanksgiving feast was held on Torquay's Daddyhole Plain to celebrate the arrival of Napoleon as a captive on HMS *Bellerophon*.

SMUGGLING

High taxes were levied on luxury goods to help finance the wars with America and France. Tea cost six times as much in Britain as it did on the continent, and brandy five times as much, and whole communities engaged in the "Free Trade", bringing in their contraband in remote coves at the dead of night, carrying it up donkey paths on precipitous cliffs and hiding it away in unlikely places. Ships returning from abroad would heave to offshore and sell exotic wares such as china, silk and cotton tax-free to the locals. More than half the spirits consumed in Britain were imported illicitly, and the activity was so profitable for France that Napoleon set up a depot for smugglers.

Old Harry's rocks were named after local pirate Harry Paye, who attacked merchant ships as they left Poole Harbour. Dorset's flat limestone reefs – a hazard to unwary sailors – were an excellent landing place for smugglers familiar with them. "French Peter" Pierre Latour worked closely with the landlord of Osmington's inn, who one day silently alerted him to a revenue man hiding in the fireplace. Latour shivered and asked for the fire to be lit. Smoked out, the terrified officer drank the brandy he was given and fled.

On Ness Beach, Beer-born Jack Rattenbury's gang carried goods through a tunnel dug in the headland, storing it in caves at Teignmouth, and Branscombe farmers dug sloping tunnels into their fields to provide further caches. Dubbed the "Rob Roy of the West", Rattenbury operated numerous enterprises on both sides of the law as well as the Channel. Mutter's Moor turf cutter Abraham Mutter distributed brandy from his fuel cart, and when Rattenbury retired to write his memoirs on a pension of a shilling a week from Lord Rolle, Abraham's brothers Sam and John headed up the gang.

In Nat Cleverly's patch at Bantham, the windows of the houses were known as "smuggler's eyes", and when he was finally caught, the magistrate hearing Cleverly's case was one of his best customers. Near Portwrinkle, Silas Finny's gang disputed his choice of landing place. The argument became so heated that Finny left, tipping off the customs officers about the next consignment. Some of the smugglers were deported to Australia under the iron rule of Captain Bligh, but those who escaped turned on Finny, whose ghost, or "gook", haunts Finnygook Inn to this day. Another smuggler to fall foul of his colleagues was curate William Penfound of Tregarfoote, who was brutally murdered in his own church.

On Cornwall's north coast, pepper and other heavily-taxed spices were hidden in the sea caves. In 1765 a Padstow resident informed the Earl of Dartmouth that in a single day his servants had encountered 60 horses travelling up from a local beach "having each three bags of tea on them of 56 or 58lbs weight".

Near Praa Sands, the self-styled "King of Prussia" and his two brothers ran a highly efficient smuggling business. Despite their illicit trade they were devout Methodists and swearing was forbidden on their ships. When Harry Carter was exiled in Brittany he preached to smugglers, and the Prussian King's scruples gave him away when he broke into Penzance Customs House to reclaim confiscated contraband. "John Carter was here," said one of the customs men. "We know it, because he has taken nothing away that was not his own." The Carters' house was auctioned in 1803 and a copper mine opened on the cliffs instead. Coal for the mine was landed in the cove, and the winch and sheds still in place were later used by the fishing fleet.

There are countless (unsubstantiated) tales of secret tunnels from beach to church or inn; but the caves beneath Hurlstone Point really were linked to Selworthy's whitewashed church, and tunnels from Bigbury did lead to Ringmore's inn, where the town council met, and to the Pilchard Inn on Burgh Island, where smuggler Tom Crocker was shot dead by a customs man.

Customs officers, too, had their share of "accidents", like Branscombe's John Hurley, "an active and diligent officer," according to his epitaph. "As he was endeavouring to extinguish some fire made between Beer and Seaton as a signal to a smuggling boat then off the sea he

POLPERRO CAVE

Polperro smuggler Willie Wilcox drowned in a cave when the tide came in as he hid from customs men. Here the Free Trade was masterminded by Zephaniah Job, who also ran several legitimate businesses. Acting as banker to the smugglers, he hired lawyers to represent them in court, sending them money in prison. On smuggling nights, Talland's vicar could be seen leaping around the churchyard, cracking a whip "to drive away evil spirits", and a brandy keg from a bungled landing near Lansallos found its way into the Wheal Howell mineshafts, causing mayhem in the mine that day.

fell by some means or other from the top of the Cliff to the bottom by which he was unfortunately killed."

The Board of Customs was established to eradicate smuggling. Certain goods could only be imported in particular places and customs officers patrolled the ports. The Revenue's sloops were upgraded to bigger, faster cutters when they proved to be no match for the smugglers' boats, and by 1782 there were there were 700 crewmen with 200 guns serving on 40 vessels. The Coast Blockade Service was formed in 1816, and 15 years later there were 6700 men in the newly streamlined Coastguard Service. Cottages were built above the coast where they could keep a lookout, and they patrolled the cliffs on the footpaths that today form stretches of the South West Coast Path.

Lundy Island provided useful warehousing for tobacco smuggled in by owner Thomas Benson, Sheriff of Devon and MP for Barnstaple. He also diverted convicts being deported to the New World on his ships, landing them instead on the island, where he used them as slaves. On the North Devon coast, conditions were so rough that the revenue men scarcely bothered with its isolated coves, making them the ideal landing place for contraband – usually goods originating in the West Indies. A rumour that human flesh was preserved in barrels in caves around the Clovelly coastline protected the goods from interfering busybodies. Further north, booty discovered by a customs officer in a Lee Bay outhouse included 66 bottles of gin, 13 gallons of Portuguese red wine, 250lbs of salt and 73 packs of playing cards, all missing the Ace of Spades (the card that was taxed).

WRECK AND RESCUE

Villager Davis Gilbert was so distressed by the bodies left on the shoreline after the 1807 HMS *Anson* shipwreck that he sought help from Helston MP Thomas Grylls and Morwenstow's Reverend Hawker to get an Act of Parliament passed, requiring all shipwreck victims to be given a Christian burial. Equally horrified at what he saw, Helston's Henry Trengrouse became obsessed with finding a way to save lives when a ship ran aground. His breeches buoy, or rocket apparatus, used a cannon to fire a double line out to a floundering ship to haul men shore, and it was adopted around the coastline. In the 1860s the Admiralty built a coastguard observation post at Gara Rock, with a "Life Saving Apparatus House", and after the SS *Uppingham* went down near Hartland Quay, the 1890 Rocket House was built for the rocket wagon and equipment of the Hartland Life Saving Apparatus Company. Prawle's volunteer Life Saving Apparatus Company was formed in

LOE BAR MEMORIAL
120 men were lost when HMS *Anson* was wrecked off Loe Bar in 1807, on its way to join a navy blockade during the Napoleonic Wars. When a sudden storm blew up, for three days the ship was stranded off the Lizard, being forced towards the bar. In desperation the captain gave orders that the ship should be run full tilt at the shingle to beach her with minimal damage, but at the last minute the ship broached. The falling mast created a bridge to shore and some of the men clambered to safety, while others were hauled ashore by villagers who had come to help; but most drowned, including the captain, who died trying to save the ship's boy.

1872, and a wreck post was installed to practise using it. Other wreck posts still stand on Old Lizard Head, Baggy Point and Prussia Cove's Cudden Point.

The results of the coastline's savage reefs and sudden storms are strewn on the rocks between Minehead and Poole, and the Coast Path is punctuated with lighthouses, lifeboat stations and the occasional figurehead salvaged from a wreck. There are many tales of heroic rescues and opportunistic looters, and of coves awash with coffee, tea or indigo.

On the north coast, in bad weather the breakers acquire a force of up to 4 tons per square metre as they storm across the Atlantic. In the 1840s, when ships were being lost around the British coastline at a rate of two a day, Hartland's "Iron Coast" was estimated to have claimed a total of 200 within living memory, and Reverend Hawker wrote: "From Padstow Point to Lundy light is a watery grave by day or night".

Stepper Point's daymark tower was erected early in the nineteenth century, and Padstow's 1827 lifeboat, stationed at Hawker's Cove, was joined in 1931 by a second boat. Following the loss of a number of fishermen during a storm, Clovelly's first lifeboat station was built in 1870; but Hartland Point's 1874 lighthouse stands over the rusted remains of the Dutch coaster, *Johanna*, wrecked on the last day of 1982.

In Combe Martin bay, the *Eleanor* was wrecked in heavy seas in 1854. The same year a fishing boat managed to save the crew of a ketch caught in storms off Lynmouth Bay, although the ship sank in the shallow water at Gore Point. In 1899, when the sea was too rough to launch Lynmouth's new lifeboat to go to the aid of a ship in trouble off Porlock, the *Louisa* was hauled 13 miles overland to be launched in Porlock.

A third of the world's shipping passes Lizard Point each year, and Sir John Killigrew built its first lighthouse in 1619 but couldn't afford its maintenance, so James I introduced a toll of a ha'penny per ton for passing vessels. This was so unpopular that Killigrew's patent was withdrawn and the lighthouse demolished. So many ships were lost in the next 150 years that another was built in 1752, described by Tennyson as "the southern eyes of England".

Kilcobben's lifeboat station opened in 1961 and serves the whole Lizard. Church Cove had an auxiliary lifeboat from 1885, but launching it from the steep slipway was difficult, and in its 14 years it was only used twice. Polpeor Cove's 1859 lifeboat was launched 136 times, saving 562 lives before it closed in 1961. In 1867 a lifeboat was stationed at Cadgwith, and another at Mullion Cove, whose vicar wrote in 1873 that in just over six years nine ships had been wrecked, "with a loss of 69 lives, under Mullyon Cliffs, on a bit of coastline not more than a mile and a half in length".

The Manacles reef claimed two naval ships on the same night in 1809 and two vessels

PISTIL MEADOW

Underfoot in Pistil Meadow's peaceful tamarisk grove is the mass grave of the 207 people drowned when the military *Royal Anne* went down off Lizard Point in November 1720. Passengers included the family of Lord Belhaven, taking up his appointment as Governor of Barbados.

transporting emigrants to America in 1855 and 1898, with the loss of many lives. More than 150 vessels were lost, at a cost of 1000 lives, before Porthoustock's lifeboat station was built in 1869. In 1907, SS *Suevic* struck the Maenheere Reef, triggering the biggest rescue in the history of the RNLI. Volunteer lifeboat crews from the Lizard, Cadgwith, Coverack and Porthleven repeatedly rowed out to the ship, despite gale-force winds and thick fog, and in 16 hours they rescued all 456 passengers, including 70 babies.

Penzance was the first Cornish port to have a lifeboat, bought for 150 guineas in 1803, but after nine years of never being used it was sold to pay off a debt. Later a new lifeboat house was built; but launching the new boat required a team of horses to drag it around two sharp corners, with deep mud around the slipway at low tide. In 1908 the boat was moved to Newlyn.

In 1981 the *Union Star* got into difficulty in winds of up to 100 mph, and eight miles east of the Scilly Isles she reported engine failure. A Culdrose Sea King was unable to winch anyone to safety and in the rough seas both the *Union Star* and Mousehole's Penlee Lifeboat went down, with the loss of all lives. The old Penlee lifeboat house was preserved as a memorial, and every year Mousehole's famous Christmas lights are switched off for an hour in remembrance.

PORTLAND BILL

Between Portland Bill and the Shambles sandbank, the turbulence from the meeting of tides can be seen from the shore even on a calm day. Many ships came to grief here as they tried to reach Weymouth and Portland Harbour. In 1844 a 7m white stone obelisk was built on the headland to warn of the rock shelf extending 30m into the sea, and the current lighthouse was built in 1906, replacing the 1869 towers on the east and west coasts. Today the east coast tower is a bird observatory.

The English Channel has its own hazards. Near Weston, a white rectangle of flint high on the hillside guides ships along the East Devon coastline, and the 1881 Anvil Point Lighthouse gives a clear line to Portland Bill and guides ships into the Solent, avoiding the perilous Christchurch Ledge. Froward's daymark tower was built in 1864 to mark the entrance to Dartmouth harbour. Berry Head Lighthouse, constructed in 1906, is Britain's shortest lighthouse (5m) and yet one of the highest (58m above sea level). It was also once the deepest, with a weight dropping down a 45m shaft to turn the optic.

Salcombe's notorious Bar is less than 60cm below water at low tide and was the scene of Devon's worst lifeboat loss, when the *William & Emma* reached the Plymouth schooner aground in Lannacombe Bay, only to find that the Prawle Rocket Company had rescued its crew. The lifeboat capsized on its return journey, drowning 13.

In 1936, the German four-masted barque *Herzogin Cecilie* – winner of many grain races – ran aground on Ham Stone Rock and was towed to Starehole Bay, where she lies shrouded in seaweed. In Hope Cove, 700 were drowned in 1760 when the captain of the 90-gun warship *Ramillie* mistook Bolt Tail for Rame Head and thought he was heading for the safety of Plymouth Sound. In the Sound itself, the 660-man warship *Coronation* capsized when it was anchored off Penlee Point in rough weather in 1691.

Gribbin Head's red-and-white striped daymark tower was built in 1832 to help sailors distinguish the headland from Dodman Point and St Anthony's Head, where the 1835 lighthouse had the largest bell in Cornwall until it was replaced by a fog horn in 1954. Portmellon's 1869 lifeboat house was moved to Mevagissey in 1888; and Portloe's steep hill down to the slipway made launching the lifeboat so tricky that during one exercise she ran out of control and crashed through a shop. A new station built on the shoreline was never used in seventeen years.

When the Coastguard Service ended in 1994 and two fishermen drowned off the Lizard's Bass Point, within sight of the newly-closed coastguard lookout, the National Coastwatch Institute was formed, establishing 50 lookout stations around the British Isles, manned by volunteers.

THE EMPIRE

The 1872 Lloyd's signal station on the Lizard's Bass Point enabled ships' captains to semaphore messages to their owners. Penzance had a swing bridge to allow ships into the dry dock at Abbey Basin and Paignton had a new harbour to cope with its annual export of 40,000 hogsheads of cider. In Salcombe, oranges and lemons were brought in from the Caribbean and the Azores, and pineapples from the Bahamas and West Indies. Also imported were sugar, rum and coconuts; ebony and mahogany for furnishing ships; and exotic plants for wealthy eccentric Otto Overbeck, inventor of a pioneering electrotherapy machine "The Rejuvenator", who left his house to the National Trust on condition that it was not turned into a brothel.

Braunton's Velator Quay had up to a hundred ships visiting at any one time, with exports including local manganese ore and produce. Limestone, coal, bricks, salt and flour were brought in from Wales. The quays at Minehead and Porlock were bustling with similar goods, and on the Gannel, ore from the Great Perran Iron Lode was exchanged for Welsh coal, needed in the Truro smelting works.

Portland's 1847 military fortress Verne Citadel was built to house the convicts providing the labour for the harbour, constructed in 1849–72 at a cost of over £1m. The convicts shifted over 5m tonnes of stone, also building their own cells in the 1848 Grove Prison, which they shared with high-profile Irish Republicans. In 1855 eighty convicts were deported from here to Western Australia, and 200 civilian warders and 150 soldiers were needed to control a mutiny in 1858.

Fremington's high-grade clay was used in the Fishley and Brannam potteries, and the latter's Royal Barum ware won a medal in the 1851 Great Exhibition. Dartmouth's 1819 papermill had the largest waterwheel west of Bristol, and its high-quality paper was used for printing Dartmouth bank notes. Near Newquay, Wheal Aaron worked ochre and umber, used for waterproofing sails and colouring dyes; and Tregardock's Tudor silver mine resumed operations with a new beam engine, tunnelling inland, and in 1853-60 it produced 60 tons of lead ore, 690 ounces of silver and some copper.

Penwith's busy Kenidjack Valley boasted 50 working waterwheels, including the second biggest in the country. At Poltesco, the Signal Staff quarry factory used a massive 25ft waterwheel to cut, turn and polish serpentine products such as fonts, shop fronts, mantelpieces and vases, ferried by flat-bottomed barges to schooners waiting offshore.

In 1826, a new harbour was built in Pentewan, with a deep-cut basin and a tidal channel, and horse-drawn trams brought china clay from St Austell and tin from Polgooth, taking back coal for the mines and gasworks and Baltic timber for barrel-making. In 1874 the first locomotive arrived to take over the task. As the river began to silt up, a sand and block works was built to use the material deposited.

Trevithick's beam engine had revolutionised Cornish mining, and the world's only steam-powered example still occupying its original mine site can be seen at Levant. These were produced at Harvey's Hayle foundry, run by Trevithick's father-in-law, and the town became one of the world's leading engineering centres. In 1888 the National Explosives Company was established in Hayle's "Dynamite Towans", producing three tons of explosives daily. There was also an explosives factory at Cligga Head. Cornish miners acquired an international reputation, and their skills were in global demand.

Opposite:

FALMOUTH DOCKS

Falmouth was the Empire's second port, and an 1858 public meeting held to discuss port facilities heard that in the previous nine years 16,078 vessels had docked here, representing a registered tonnage of over 4m tons, excluding coasting vessels, which were themselves estimated at over 1m tons. Work went ahead on the new Falmouth Docks, and wharves, breakwaters and the dry dock were completed just as the Great Western Railway arrived, in 1863.

Between 1815 and 1915 up to 500,000 Cornishmen migrated abroad to meet this need. During its boom, Cornwall produced around 80% of Britain's copper and was the world's most important copper mining region. On its western coastline the rocks were seamed with almost-vertical tin and copper lodes which continued under the sea, and mines were perched perilously on clifftops to service tunnels bored many fathoms below the seabed. In an area where over 100 windlasses could be seen above mineshafts, Perranuthnoe's Trenow Consols attracted a state visit from Queen Victoria when she visited Penzance with Prince Albert. Wheal Charlotte's Trenow engine shaft had been driven to a depth of over 100m and produced ore worth over £11,000 before it closed.

Towards the end of the boom, a group of St Just miners returning from the Boer Wars in 1899 set up the Geevor Tin Mine Company, with capital from the Western Australian Gold Field Company. The largest employer in the district, Geevor ran until 1990, when the price of tin crashed from over £10,000 a ton to £3,500 a ton.

Steam technology, matched by advances in scientific discovery, was being applied across the board. In 1809 Camborne and Redruth were linked to the ports at Hayle and Portreath by a tramroad. Hayle Railway, built in 1837, incorporated four cable-operated inclined planes, using stationary steam winders to raise and lower trucks on the steep sections. In Newquay, the 1849 tram track carrying ore from East Wheal Rose to the harbour continued in use after the railway arrived in 1884, and the carriers hauling the trucks also took the Royal Mail to the post office.

Portland's 1826 horse-drawn Merchants Railway was one of the world's earliest public railways, and in 1865 it carried 81,000 tonnes of Portland stone. The Yeates Incline hauled stone uphill by means of two lines of trucks joined by a chain running over a drum, using the weight of laden trucks descending to bring the empty ones back up to the top. Teams of horses transported the stone to and from the trucks.

In 1843 Isambard Kingdom Brunel was appointed engineer to the South Devon Railway. Unlike his SS *Great Britain* and Saltash Bridge, Brunel's innovative "atmospheric railway" was dramatically unsuccessful. Pipes were run along the rails, with pumps creating a vacuum to draw the trains along them; but with no telegraph system to communicate between them, the pumping stations had to empty the pipes according to a timetable, which relied on the trains arriving on time. However, the salt spray made it difficult to seal the pipes, and rats ate the tallow seals used, so that there were frequent breakdowns, on occasion requiring the third-class passengers to help push the train. In 1848 Brunel conceded defeat, making no charge for his work, and a conventional railway was built

BOTALLACK MINE

Botallack was one of the most successful Cornish mines. Nearby, Cape Cornwall mine worked tin and copper from 1836-79, and its 1864 tower was left as a navigational landmark when it closed. Later the mine's ore dressing floors were converted to greenhouses and wineries, and eventually site owners H J Heinz donated it to the nation.

instead. Remnants of his handiwork can be seen in the pumping station at Starcross and the viaduct at Broadsands.

Another white elephant was the major defence project known as the "Palmerston Follies". Following Napoleon III's 1859 launch of the first armour-plated battleship, Prime Minister Palmerston's Royal Commission committed the country to an £11m spend on defending the Empire's arsenals and dockyards.

Plymouth was allocated £3m to protect its port and docks. Forts Stamford, Bovisand and Staddon defended the Eastern approaches, along with Breakwater Fort on Shovel Rock. Brownhill Battery, accommodating 200 men with 14 guns, covered the ground in front of the lines and the surrounding scarp, and the Battery at Staddon Heights protected shipping at the mouth of the Sound. Fort Turnchapel covered the area from the merchant ship anchorage at Jennycliff Bay to the north flank of Staddon Fort.

At St Anthony Head, a battery of 24-pounder guns protected Carrick Roads, enclosed by high ramparts with an unclimbable iron fence and manned by the Stannary Regiment.

TREGANTLE

The most westerly defence in a chain of more than 20 forts and batteries ringing Plymouth, Tregantle accommodated 2000 men and was designed for 35 guns; but the 32-pounder installed in 1882 was the only gun, needing just six gunners to operate it. Other forts defending Plymouth's Western flank were built at Scraesdon, Cawsand, Polhawn and Picklecombe, interspersed with batteries and other gun emplacements and linked by the military road. New batteries were established at Mount Edgcumbe and on Maker Heights, where there was also a military hospital. The 1863 Garden Battery covered the channel to Plymouth Dockyard between West Hoe and Drake's Island. One of the earliest (and largest) guns at Penlee Battery was hauled into position by 80 horses, taking two weeks to arrive and splitting its concrete bed on the first firing. On the shoreline below, the Pier Cellars Brennan torpedo station was built in 1888–89.

PORTLAND HIGH ANGLE BATTERY

With an allocation of £630,000 (sixth on Palmerston's list), Portland's defences included Breakwater and Nothe Forts, built by convicts. Verne Citadel was extended to accommodate the troops working the East Weare Battery below it, and the 1892 Verne high-angle battery housed six 12-ton guns deep within a quarry, angled at 70° to rain down on to enemy ships' decks. Another high-angle battery at Rame Head protected Plymouth Sound.

Fowey's two 64-pounder guns at St Catherine's Castle, modified in 1855 during the Crimean War, were manned by Artillery Volunteers.

In 1895 the Mevagissey Electric Supply Company built a power station to burn the oil pressed from pilchards, and Lynmouth's hydro-electric power station was the first in the world to use off-peak electricity to pump water back up to its reservoir to be re-used.

In 1860 an undersea cable was laid from Dartmouth's Compass Cove to Guernsey, with another to Jersey in 1877, sending messages via electrical pulses. Later the cable ran underground to a repeater station in an old coach house, sending transatlantic communications. In 1870, the Empire's first submarine cable ran from Porthcurno to India via Portugal, with further links all over the globe. In 1897, Marconi's Wireless Telegraph Company was established, sending radio signals to the Isle of Wight from the roof of Durlston Castle before doing the same from Poldhu in 1901. At the end of that year he transmitted the first transatlantic radio signals from Poldhu to Newfoundland. Porthcurno was the hub of international cable communications for the next 100 years and the largest cable station in the world. Its 14 cables used the binary code underpinning the internet, and it remains the landing point for international cable networks.

As well as providing transport links for industry, the South West's new railways brought tourism to the region. Instow's railway arrived in 1855, two years before Bridport's, which was extended to West Bay in 1884 – the year Newquay's railway brought a tourist boom to Cornwall. Paignton's rail connection was greeted in 1859 by mini riots, caused by a rare public baking of the enormous thirteenth-century "Paignton Pudding". Westward Ho! was a big hit with tourists after Charles Kingsley's bestselling novel in 1855, and the Bideford, Westward Ho! and Appledore Railway ran sightseeing trips around the coast from Bideford. On the Bristol Channel, Minehead and Lynmouth became places to "take the waters", and Ilfracombe's 1874 railway attracted pleasure steamers too. Here, Rapparee was a "ladies only" beach, and the men's and ladies' Tunnels Beaches were accessed separately through tunnels blasted by Welsh miners. In Torquay, Agatha Christie spent childhood beach holidays in the "ladies only" Beacon Cove.

Lady Ada Lovelace, Byron's daughter, had Swiss mountaineers construct tunnels to her own private beach at Ashley Combe, above Porlock Weir. She is credited with devising the world's first software, arising from promenades in the terraced gardens of her fairytale mansion with computer guru Charles Babbage.

The countless writers and artists inspired by the coastline include Thomas Hardy, who courted his wife Emma in the Boscastle area; poets Shelley and Tennyson; R D Blackmore,

LYNMOUTH CLIFF RAILWAY

In 1890, George Newnes (publisher of the Sherlock Holmes stories) built a cliff railway linking Lynmouth and Lynton, powered by water gravity-fed from the River Lyn and still the world's only carbon-neutral railway. Oddicombe's cliff railway was not built until 1923, after Newnes failed to get permission for it, but he was a key figure in the 1898 Lynton-Barnstaple Railway and responsible for several public buildings in Lynton. His Hollerday House was burnt down in mysterious circumstances, after a family feud between himself and the Hallidays of nearby Glenthorne. Reverend Walter Halliday – a collaborator on the railway project – had inherited a large fortune from his family in Scotland, on condition that he should use it to establish a country estate, which he did at Glenthorne, inspired by Wordsworth's poetry, which he quoted above the door of his fishing lodge at Watersmeet.

whose Lorna Doone was set at Oare; Charles Dickens, whose "Steepways" was based on Clovelly; Millais, whose "The Boyhood of Raleigh" celebrated Budleigh Salterton; Constable, who painted Bowleaze Cove; Dylan Thomas, whose Llareggub in "Under Milk Wood" was inspired by Mousehole; landscape artist Thomas Creswick of the Birmingham School of artists, who painted Rocky Valley's Trevillet Mill; and Samuel Palmer, whose

CARBIS BAY ARTISTS

After two years' study in France, where there was a thriving art colony in Pont Aven, artist Stanhope Forbes arrived in Penzance in 1884, looking for something similar in Cornwall. He and his wife, Elizabeth, settled in Newlyn, establishing the post-Impressionist Newlyn School of artists, which included S.J. "Lamorna" Birch. Attracted by Penwith's remoteness, scenic beauty, quality of life and pure light, a steady stream of artists followed him. In 1890 they founded the Newlyn Industrial Class, specialising in domestic items in copper and designed to provide work when fishing was slack; and in 1895 the Newlyn Art Gallery opened, one of 70 buildings funded by Cornish philanthropist John Passmore Evans. A similar community of artists was later established in St Ives, when Cedric Morris and Christopher Wood moved in and "discovered" Alfred Wallis, who painted seascapes "for company" after his wife died. Potter Bernard Leach based himself here and designed a series of floor tiles on a fishing theme for St Nicholas Chapel on St Ives Head, refurbished following a public outcry when the War Office partly demolished it in 1904.

"Scene from Lee" hangs in Cambridge's Fitzwilliam Museum. The adventures of Georgeham-based Henry Williamson's *Tarka the Otter* took place around North Devon.

Brunel's brother-in-law, who lived near him in Watcombe, was commissioned to design a Christmas card, and in 1843 the first commercial batch of 1000 cards sold at one shilling each. Welcombe's Hermitage was used as a retreat by priests from London's Brompton Oratory, and Deep Purple wrote one of their most successful albums there.

Coleton Fishacre was the holiday home of the D'Oyly Carte family. It is one of a number of Art Deco buildings built around the coastline, including Saunton Sands Hotel, the Burgh Island Hotel and Penzance's Yacht Inn, sited opposite the Art Deco Jubilee Pool with Cubist-style diving platforms. The 30-acre garden at Fishacre is one of many where sub-tropical and tropical plants thrive in the warm, moist air – as they do at Carwinion, Trebah and Glendurgan on the Helford River, and in George's Burt's Durlston and the Fox-Strangways' Abbotsbury Subtropical Gardens. South Devon's Blackpool Gardens were established in 1896 by the Deputy Governor of the Bank of England, one of the two men responsible for financing Britain in the First World War, and today include the National Magnolia Collection.

Cornish architect and philanthropist Silvanus Trevail built imposing Gothic hotels in Newquay and Tintagel, and Tregardock's Gothic school buildings were inspired by a Trevail drawing. Like Prussia Cove's Porth-en-Alls House, Bridport's parish church was built in the Arts and Crafts style, rebelling against mass production, and one of the movement's leading artists, John Ruskin, saved Parracombe's old parish church from demolition when it was replaced by a modern one.

The Victorian love of romance inspired a number of follies around the coastline, including the Kimmeridge Clavell Tower and Bude's Tower of the Winds, both built in the 1830s, as well as Lee Abbey's Duty Point Tower. Sir Thomas Acland built a wind and weather hut in the extensive woodlands he planted on Bossington Hill, where he set out miles of footpaths for public enjoyment.

George Burt built an enormous globe using limestone from his quarries, and brought back a number of unwanted London landmarks as ballast in his ships, including the Wellington Clock Tower in 1867. Sidmouth's Alma Bridge (named after the 1854 Crimean battle) was built using timbers from a local shipwreck.

Piers and pavilions were built in seaside resorts, with terraces of elegant villas for the landed gentry's summer holidays, and promenades, gardens, theatres and assembly rooms for their delectation. They laid out carriageways in their country estates, too: Lord Revelstoke's ran for nine miles, while Flete's ran both sides of the river to teahouses on the beach at Mothecombe and Westcombe. At Peppercombe the Pine-Coffin family's prefabricated beach bungalow painted in the GWR rum-and-raisin livery was transported in sections by horse and cart.

Times were hard at the other end of the social spectrum. Formed in 1794 but disbanded after Napoleon's defeat, the Dorset Volunteer Rangers were reformed in 1830 to deal with the unrest among poverty-stricken farmworkers poaching and stealing sheep after the harvest failed. Two years later a cholera epidemic swept through Penwith, and victims were buried in a mass grave in Penzance's parish church. Despite this, as well as several disastrous mackerel seasons, the people of Newlyn funded the Ebenezer Primitive Methodist Chapel in 1835. Another cholera epidemic hit Mevagissey in 1849, and some 200 victims were quarantined in tents on a Portmellon hillside. In 1891, the South West suffered unusually badly in the Great Blizzard, and 200 people and 6000 animals were killed.

The zigzag paths on Ilfracombe's Capstone Hill were built by unemployed labourers, as was Torquay's Rock Walk. As Cornwall's pilchard stocks began to dry up in the 1890s, Lord Robartes of Lanhydrock funded a new harbour at Mullion to enable fishermen to catch crabs and lobsters instead. At Buck's Mills, as the herring and mackerel died out, the fishermen commuted daily to Lundy Island to work in its quarries.

The mines were struggling now, too, as new reserves of copper were extracted much more cheaply in South American mines, which did not need the extensive pumping required by Cornwall's waterlogged shafts. A further slump in the value of lead, zinc and tin closed many mines, and charities such as the Dorcas Society provided clothes and bedding for the needy, while Lamp societies raised funds to install gas lighting.

The Royal National Mission to Deep Sea Fishermen began its missionary service in 1881 in the North Sea, and its land-based mission in Newlyn was so successful that in 1911, following a donation from Nora Bolitho, the Ship Institute was founded to provide support and comfort for fishing families.

DOLLY PENTREATH
Cornwall's Celtic tongue finally died out in the nineteenth century. In 1860 Napoleon's nephew Louis Lucien Bonaparte erected a monument to Paul's Dolly Pentreath, said to be the last fluent speaker of the language, although Boswednack schoolmaster John Davey was said to be able to converse in it a few decades later.

On Wembury's Mewstone, warrener Sam Wakeham had a vegetable garden and kept chickens and a couple of pigs. He supplemented his meagre living with a spot of smuggling, as well as a ferry service "to the Moonstone, for anyone on the mainland who holds up their white pockethanchecuffs for a signal".

Near Lamorna, in today's Kemyel Crease Nature Reserve, Victorian gardeners planted stands of hardy Monterey pine and cypress to provide some shelter for small gardens enclosed by fuchsia hedges, where donkeys were used to till the soil and carry up seaweed for fertiliser. There were more than a hundred of these "quillets", and their flowers and potatoes ripened much earlier than anywhere else in Britain, thanks to the mild climate and the well-drained south-facing cliffs. These were sent by rail to London until the 1930s. Potatoes, flowers, fruit and corn were grown in Branscombe's Weston Plats, similar south-facing parcels of land sheltered by high cliffs and watered by a spring, and "Branscombe spuds" were also harvested early. Like the lawnsheds on Portland, the plats were passed down through the generations.

Most villagers had allotments. At Polperro, fishermen grew vegetables on the cliffs alongside "Reuben's Walk", named after a local magistrate who liked to stroll to the lighthouse even after his eyesight had failed.

In 1902, quick-firing guns were established on Falmouth's Crab Quay for use against fast torpedo boats, and a new battery was built on St Anthony Head. Appledore shipyard's last wooden merchant ship was launched in 1912, and then the "Iron Yard" started building the riveted wrought-iron vessels which were much in demand as shipping losses rose alarmingly during hostilities in the First World War.

THE WORLD AT WAR

In 1914, Lawrence Binyon sat on the cliffs at Padstow's Pentire Point and wrote "For the Fallen", which *The Times* published that September. The same year, pioneer aviator Henri Salmet landed his aircraft on Minehead Beach, heralding a new age of air transport. During the First World War, biplanes were based at Prawle Point, watching for enemy vessels, and there were RNAS seaplanes in Torbay and RAF Cattewater, which was also a base for high-speed air sea rescue launches, whose research staff later included Lawrence of Arabia.

Five army camps were built on Ballard Down and a tank training camp established at Bovington, with a gunnery range at Lulworth. The Bideford, Westward Ho! and Appledore tourist railway was closed when its rolling stock was requisitioned for the war effort, and

Porlock Weir's village hall was originally a WWI military building. There was an observation post on Prussia Cove's Cudden Point, where HMS *Warspite* was later wrecked on her way to the scrapyard after seeing service in both world wars. On Hartland Point, there is a memorial to the 162 men who died in 1918 when a German torpedo sank a steamship fully illuminated as a hospital ship that the enemy claimed was carrying arms to France.

After the war, the government's decision to build "Homes fit for heroes" led to the 1930 Slums Clearance Act, which sentenced Newlyn's cramped seafront buildings to demolition as a new council estate was built at the top of Chywoon Hill. The fishermen, who now had to toil up a steep hill with all their gear, took a petition by fishing boat to the Minister of Housing, who met them with saffron buns and pasties and gave their cottages a stay of execution.

Other 1930s housing plans provoked uproar. A speculator bought a large part of Pentire Point, offering building plots for sale, but public opposition was sufficient for the National Trust to buy all the land. This later led to the Trust's 1965 Neptune Coastline Campaign, which has since acquired more than 700 miles of coastline in England, Wales and Northern Ireland.

Penarvon Cove was donated to the Trust in 1971 by the daughters of Colonel C.F. Jerram, who had been so outraged at the "For Sale" sign he spotted there when sailing up the Helford River in 1926 that he bought the 34 acres, building a single bungalow for his own use. In Studland, the Bankes family failed to stop the development of the Glebeland estate when the agent they sent to the auction missed the train. Plans for extensive building at Exmoor's Sherrycombe came to nothing, as did ambitious town plans at Crackington Haven.

At Trevelgue, in 1933 the 40 acres of "Trebelsue Big Field" hosted a national aviation display, and six years later Western Airways moved in to run twice-daily flights linking Newquay with St Just, Barnstaple and Swansea. In 1939 RAF Trebelsue became a satellite airfield for RAF St Eval and was a target for several enemy bombing raids during 1941. Two years later RAF St Mawgan was constructed.

Once again the South West coastline was armed to guard the vital ports and repel any possible invasion. The remnants of concrete blocks and other barriers can still be seen on many of the beaches and clifftops around the South West, as can the remains of a concrete boat, abandoned in Labrador Bay after D-Day. The guns at St Anthony Head were remounted, manned by the Territorials, and at Rosemullion there was an emplacement for anti-aircraft guns with searchlights. Fowey's blockhouse became the firing point for a

PORTHCURNO TUNNELS

There was uproar at Porthcurno in 1826, when the 80-ton Logan Rock topping the Treryn Dinas Iron Age fort was dislodged by a group of sailors led by Oliver Goldsmith's nephew. The Admiralty was obliged to restore it to its original position, at a cost of £130 8s 6d, using 60 men and 13 capstans, with blocks and chains from the dockyard at Plymouth. Across the cove, Rowena Cade's 1932 Minack Theatre was less controversial. The daughter of a Derbyshire cotton mill owner and great-great-granddaughter of Joseph Wright, the "painter of the Industrial Revolution", Cade did much of the heavy construction work herself. Just 100 miles from Brest, Porthcurno's critical cable station was vulnerable to enemy attack in WW2, and Cornish miners dug a network of tunnels to protect the undersea cables and associated equipment.

controlled minefield laid across the mouth of the estuary, and the batteries at St Catherine's Castle saw action again.

Wembury Point Holiday Camp was transformed into the Cambridge Gunnery School, replacing the 1856 HMS *Cambridge*, and Maker Heights was again a key location. Further north, Southern Command's coastal defences included batteries at Instow and Appledore, and Minehead's pier was demolished to provide better visibility for the harbour's batteries. There were gun emplacements on Mutters Moor, with lookout posts and barrage balloons, and at Brandy Head the Exeter-based RAF Gunnery Research Unit established a range to test new aircraft-mounted cannon and gun sights, with targets placed out in the bay for Typhoons, Hurricanes and Spitfires. Ballard Down was used as a firing range for fighter pilot training, and the War Cabinet took over Tyneham village and the surrounding area, issuing a compulsory purchase order in 1948 to continue weapons training long-term. Tyneham House became an administrative centre for the radar station at Brandy Bay, part of a long-range general navigation system.

There was an increase in operational flying from Mount Batten, which suffered a number of German air raids, and Predannack was a forward base for Hurricanes and Spitfires. There

PORLOCK PILLBOX
Each of Porlock's WW2 pillboxes was designed for eight or nine men armed with light machine guns and rifles, with loopholes placed to protect the other pillboxes as well as the land behind. There were observation posts and pillboxes right around the coastline, many of them used for the remote detonation of mines laid to protect waterways and harbours. Post-war, pillboxes in Torquay and on the River Otter were refurbished as bat roosts.

was an airfield at Cligga Head, and Chivenor's civil airfield became an RAF Coastal Command Station in 1940. Treligga's glider airfield was commandeered by the Admiralty for use as an aerial bombing and gunnery range, staffed by the Women's Royal Naval Service. In 1943 an American pilot made a successful emergency landing here just yards from the Wrens' quarters after a raid on U-boats at Nantes.

Torridge shipyards were commissioned to turn out wooden mine sweepers, as steel hulls were vulnerable to magnetic mines, and the secluded location of the estuary made it a good place for testing top-secret weapons and equipment. Galmpton's yard built wooden motor torpedo boats, and there was a military boat repairing facility at Dartmouth. Near Looe, Watergate's new boatyard stood on land reclaimed for the purpose; and Portmellon boatbuilder Percy Mitchell built motor cutters for the Admiralty, after his Mevagissey fishing lugger caught a record-breaking 2346 stones of pilchards.

Portland was a target for heavy bombing, although most of the warships had moved away to avoid it. Bude's Maer Down is pitted with bomb craters from its days as a WW2 practice range, while in Aveton Gifford the enterprising villagers used their bomb crater as a tidal swimming pool. Mount Edgcumbe was gutted by incendiary bombs and rebuilt by the sixth Earl. In Porlock eight US airmen died when their Liberator bomber ploughed into Bossington Hill in thick fog; but in a separate incident a German pilot managed to crash land his plane on the beach despite having been intercepted by three Spitfires

Falmouth's docks were a prime target for enemy air raids, and decoys were established on the neighbouring coastline. At Nare Point, Ealing Studios built a film set featuring red and green lights to mimic the docks and train depot. Controlled remotely from a bunker on Lestowder Cliff, the studio also mocked up an open door and a poorly shaded window, using tar barrels, cordite flashes and paraffin fires to suggest successful hits on "the docks". The lake behind Polridmouth Beach was used to simulate Fowey harbour and a second decoy site was established at Nare Head. When enemy aircraft were spotted, Falmouth's lights were switched off and one of the decoy sites lit up instead.

The Secret Intelligence Service established a Helford Flotilla to maintain clandestine contact with its networks in Brittany. With a forward base in the Scilly Isles, the flotilla used fast motor launches and Breton fishing boats to run frequent nocturnal missions to isolated French beaches, infiltrating agents and collecting downed airmen.

US and Canadian troops used North Hill, between Minehead and Porlock, for tank training. Their Shermans and Churchills were unloaded in the marshalling area in Moor Wood, where ramps and concrete "devil's teeth" can still be seen. The high road and several tracks on the ridge were constructed for tanks to drive to the training areas on Bossington Hill and around Brockholes. Here dugouts provided observation posts and gun emplacements, and three short rail tracks delivered moving targets for firing practice.

Burton Bradstock's US and Canadian troops were brought in to help defend the coastline identified by Hitler as the ideal landing spot. Joint training with British commandos in advance of D-Day included climbing practice on Hive Beach, preparing them to scale the Normandy cliffs to disable enemy guns. Portland Castle, too, was used for D-Day preparations.

On Braunton Burrows the old ferry way from Lobb to Crow Point was widened and straightened for US vehicles, with training ramps built in the dunes, and Croyde Bay was used for troop practice with amphibious vehicles. Assault practice took place around Baggy Point and Woolacombe Beach – also a demolition training area – and Morte Point hosted target practice for seaborne artillery and anti-tank guns. Backed by dunes and tidal inlets but sheltered from Atlantic breakers, Instow Beach was an important training area for landing practice, and US troops were billeted in the big houses along the seafront in 1943. Fremington Training Camp was built as a hospital and rehabilitation centre, later a launching site for amphibious DUKWs on both sides of the estuary, and there was a small minefield on Northam Burrows.

A concrete slipway was built across Salcombe's Mill Bay to prepare and maintain landing craft, and in the lead-up to D-Day Churchill is said to have met with Eisenhower in the Burgh Island Hotel, designated a convalescent centre for wounded RAF personnel.

In 1943, the Slapton area's 3000 villagers were evacuated for US forces to practise landings, and in April 1944 nine tank landing ships carrying 30,000 troops set off on a circuit around Lyme Bay for a mock assault on Slapton Sands. They were attacked by German E-boats, and three of the landing ships were hit. Hundreds of men were drowned, while others were killed by the friendly fire designed to make Exercise Tiger as realistic as possible. Today a Sherman tank recovered from the seabed stands at Torcross as a memorial to those who died.

In the last enemy air raid of the war, a large fuel depot behind Swanpool was hit. A torrent of fuel earmarked for D-Day flowed through the valley towards the houses below. A quick-witted US Navy officer diverted it at the last moment using a bulldozer and was later awarded the British Empire Medal.

On St Aldhelm's Head there is a monument marking the area's WW2 radar research. Renscombe Down, near Chapman's Pool, was the nerve centre of the UK's radar

BROWNSTONE BATTERY

Hitler's 1940 Operation Sealion invasion plan targeted Lyme Bay, with Bridport and Hive Beach as his ideal landing spots. Britain's "Stop Line" stretched from Bridport to Portland, with numerous lookouts, gun emplacements and pillboxes built above the shoreline. Near Kingswear, Brownstone Battery was built to prevent enemy forces from landing at Slapton or Blackpool Sands.

development during the war. Early radar work operated on the Suffolk coast and then Dundee before relocating here, where the high flat terrain is ideal for radar and the site was further from any potential Nazi invasion. In 1940, some 200 staff moved into Worth Matravers, initially developing the rotating aerial and map display used for target-tracking and then designing systems with a longer range, for aircraft navigation. In 1942 a British paratrooper raid secured key components from a German radar installation on the French coast, and Renscombe's by now 2000-strong workforce was relocated to Malvern in case of reprisals.

St Aldhelm's Head was one of 21 coastal Early Warning RDF (Radio Direction Finding) stations located around the eastern seaboard, with two 240ft masts near the village and a further site on the clifftop to detect low-flying aircraft. After the war the base was used by the RAF as a training station.

There were other radio and radar stations around Purbeck, including Durlston's Oboe radio navigation station, codenamed Tilly Whim, and a Coastal Defence (CD) on Swanage Down for detecting ships. Nine Barrow Down's VHF radio communications masts were particularly important following damage to the planned undersea telephone cable link during the D-Day landings.

Hartland Point was a naval VHF intercept station for the "Y service", jointly operated by the Army, Royal Navy, the RAF, the Foreign Office, the Metropolitan Police and the GPO and a feeder service for the Enigma operation. Later it became a Chain Home Low radar station, boosting low-level coverage in association with the local station on Northam Burrows to plot surface shipping and low-flying aircraft. At Rame Head, as well as a Ground Controlled Interception hut the Chain station had a bunker thought to have been part of an anti-submarine acoustic listening network.

Post-war there was a need for more sophisticated equipment to cope with the high speed of approaching aircraft, and Chain Home sites became Cold War Rotor sites. One was built on the Exmoor coast at West Myne in the 1950s and was in use until 1964, when the site was levelled.

Above Duckpool, the bowls and balls of the British signals intelligence service (GCHQ) radio station occupy the former RAF Cleave airfield. Operated jointly by UK and USA staff, it intercepts and analyses signals for the Echelon intelligence network on behalf of the five signatory states to the 1946 UK/USA "Five Eyes" Security Agreement, which formalised the 1941 intelligence-sharing agreement of the Atlantic Charter, defining the Allied goals for the post-war world.

VERYAN COLD WAR BUNKER
As advancing technology made the old forts and batteries obsolete, most were decommissioned or replaced by the high-tech installations which were themselves made redundant as a new age opened in the history of the coastline. Today the National Trust owns the once top-secret nuclear bunker near Veryan. Built in 1963 and manned by the Royal Observer Corps, the Cold War underground post was designed to detect nuclear bursts and monitor subsequent radioactivity. It was declared redundant in a 1991 spending review. A few miles away, RAF Treleaver's 1953 GCI Rotor Radar Station closed in 1958, and today a brewery occupies its upper floor while the radar plinths house chickens.

THE SOUTH WEST COAST PATH

By the middle of the twentieth century, South West England's economic heritage had ground to a halt. The sea had been fished out, the mines put out of business by foreign competition, and land and air transport systems had sidelined its maritime traditions, including its once-critical location as a front-line defence. The only card left in its hand was its breathtaking beauty, and so tourism became its mainstay.

In 1935, walker and journalist Tom Stephenson wrote a *Daily Herald* article entitled "Wanted: A Long Green Trail", mooting the idea of a long-distance walking route through the Pennines. He envisioned "a faint line on the Ordnance Maps, which the feet of grateful pilgrims would, with the passing years, engrave on the face of the land." The Ramblers Association was formed the same year, and Stephenson became its secretary, writing the first guide to the Pennine Way when it was finally established in 1965.

The Labour Government's post-war reconstruction of the UK included the 1949 National Parks and Access to the Countryside Act, which addressed public rights of way and access to open land and received all-party support. The creation of a path around the South West peninsula, based on the clifftop footpaths beaten out by nineteenth-century Customs Officers in pursuit of smugglers, was one of the first of the new long distance routes to be identified. The North Cornwall section was the first to be designated, in 1952, with the final section in Dorset designated in 1963. However, the long process of negotiation of consultation and negotiation with landowners to fill in the gaps meant that it wasn't until the opening of the Somerset and North Devon section, in 1978, that the South West Coast Path as a National Trail came into being.

It has since grown in popularity and is rated as one of the world's greatest hikes. Although incredibly popular, with over 8.6 million tourist visits a year, and probably at least that many walks taken on it by local people, if you choose your spot and when you go, you can still find peace and tranquillity.

Today it is maintained by a dedicated team of rangers and wardens working for the County Councils and National Trust, coordinated by the South West Coast Path team, with increasing support from the volunteers, staff and funds raised by the South West Coast Path Association – a charity dedicated to conserve and protect the Path.